Beginning
with
GOD

A Basic Introduction to
the Christian Faith

EXPANDED
EDITION

JAMES W. SIRE

IVP Books

An imprint of InterVarsity Press
Downers Grove, Illinois

InterVarsity Press
P.O. Box 1400, Downers Grove, IL 60515-1426
ivpress.com
email@ivpress.com

InterVarsity Press® is the book-publishing division of InterVarsity Christian Fellowship/USA®, a
movement of students and faculty active on campus at hundreds of universities, colleges, and
schools of nursing in the United States of America, and a member movement of the International
Fellowship of Evangelical Students. For information about local and regional activities, visit
intervarsity.org.

All Scripture quotations, unless otherwise indicated, are taken from THE HOLY BIBLE, NEW
INTERNATIONAL VERSION®, NIV® Copyright © 1973, 1978, 1984, 2011 by Biblica, Inc.™
Used by permission. All rights reserved worldwide.

While any stories in this book are true, some names and identifying information
may have been changed to protect the privacy of individuals.

Cover design: Cindy Kiple
Interior design: Daniel van Loon
Images: branch leaves: © cat_arch_angel/iStockphoto

ISBN 978-0-8308-4505-7 (print)
ISBN 978-0-8308-9096-5 (digital)

Printed in the United States of America ∞

Library of Congress Cataloging-in-Publication Data

Names: Sire, James W., author.

Title: Beginning with God : a basic introduction to the Christian faith /
    James W. Sire.

Description: Expanded Edition. | Downers Grove : InterVarsity Press, 2017. |
    Includes bibliographical references.

Identifiers: LCCN 2017010363 (print) | LCCN 2017016608 (ebook) | ISBN
    9780830890965 (eBook) | ISBN 9780830845057 (pbk. : alk. paper)

Subjects: LCSH: Theology, Doctrinal—Popular works.

Classification: LCC BT77 (ebook) | LCC BT77 .S56 2017 (print) | DDC 230—dc23

LC record available at https://lccn.loc.gov/2017010363

P	18	17	16	15	14	13	12	11	10	9	8	7	6	5	4	3	2	1
Y	33	32	31	30	29	28	27	26	25	24	23	22	21	20	19	18	17	

To Richard and Ann and their friends at First Presbyterian Church who have confirmed their faith in Jesus Christ

Contents

Preface

I WAS RIDING MY PONY early one summer evening, driving the milk cows from the high pasture back to the ranch in the valley below. I must have been ten years old. Far away three huge thunderclouds began pushing their heads higher and higher over the western horizon. The declining sun was hidden. The air turned cool and electric. I was half a mile from home and struck with the awesome sensation that I was being pursued by the Father, the Son, and the Holy Ghost.

From such experiences of the "holy" stemmed my early interest in the Christian faith. Hardly biblical, but a start. A few years later, with a bit better grasp on the good news of Jesus Christ, I became a Christian.

Even after this I felt uncertain about my faith for years. I didn't doubt that God was real. I knew that he had done something new in my life. But I couldn't explain what Christianity was all about. I didn't know where to begin. I didn't know where to end. And I didn't know what went in between. I have described much of this pilgrimage in *Rim of the Sandhills* (ebook, 2012).

It took many years for these matters to become clear in my own mind. Now I realize that in explaining the good news we can start anywhere. We can begin with a deep philosophic issue (like the problem of evil) or with the simple, longing cry of a hurting father wondering why his son has played the prodigal. We can begin with the wonders of the star-studded universe, the beauty of a mountain lake, or the corruption of city government, the decadence of Broadway in San Francisco, or even the flight of two 767s into the World Trade Center buildings of New York.

Of course, the story really begins with God. But the feeling that we need to hear such a story begins with us. And that's where this book begins—with our wonderment about who we are as men and women.

My overall goal is to set forth the central teaching of the Christian faith. I believe that as Christians we should concentrate on those doctrines that are commonly held by Christians at all times and in all places. C. S. Lewis called this "mere Christianity." So in what follows I have focused on the basic, essential teachings of Scripture.

Every book has its origin somewhere in the life of its writer. This book is a spinoff from a task I was assigned as an elder of First United Presbyterian

Church of Downers Grove. During an interim between pastors, I was asked to teach the confirmation class. While my church had some material
for this purpose, I felt it would not fit our needs.
As a result, I prepared a series of studies that students would work on prior to each week's class.
The questions at the end of each chapter of this
book have their source there.

After teaching this class for several years, it oc-
curred to me that these studies in basic Christianity
might be useful to readers beyond our
denomination—perhaps to those teaching confirmation or adult membership classes where it is
important to survey the essentials of the faith. After
the first edition was published in 1981, it became
a foundational text for confirmation classes and
has remained so for thirty years.

The chapters are organized around a simple
scheme: creation, the fall, redemption, new life in
Christ, and glorification. This is, I believe, the
pattern of biblical theology. Moreover, it leads
readers to consider their own status before God.
Chapter ten on what it means to be "born again"
gives direct help to those who wish for the first
time to commit their lives to Jesus.

It is my hope—no, my prayer—that readers
who have yet to believe will find this book a step
along the way to sincere faith in God.

Three reservations. First, this book does not pretend to be an apologetic for Christianity. I do not attempt to argue for the truth of the faith. Rather, I have tried simply to expose the central teaching of the Bible. Of course, this in itself is an apologetic, for truth has a way of convincing the sincere searcher.

Second, I want readers to know that there are many other explanations of the faith. If you are not a Christian and this explanation does not appeal to you, please do not abandon your quest on the basis of what I say. Search the Scriptures on your own. And try other books that attempt the same primary goal as this one. John Stott's *Basic Christianity* is my prime recommendation. His presentation focuses on the life, character, and teaching of Jesus as recorded in the Gospels, while mine is more explicitly theological and based on Paul's letters.

Third, as will become obvious, this book only scratches the surface of a very complex subject. Notes to most chapters are found at the back of the book. They not only provide documentation for some of the remarks made in the chapters but also often suggest further reading.

Finally, a word to those who choose to use this book as a basis for group discussion. The study questions at the end of each chapter are designed to stimulate thought and to focus on key ideas in the chapter. They may form a basis for group discussion. Each leader, however, will wish to revise, abridge, and supplement these to fit the particular group situation.

I wish to acknowledge the stimulus and challenge of students in my confirmation class over the course of seven years. I also acknowledge the suggestions of subsequent confirmation class teachers who have used material from this book. They join me in commending readers to take a good look at what being truly human really means.

CHAPTER ONE

What's in a Name?

> "Tell me your name and your business," [said Humpty Dumpty].
>
> "My *name* is Alice, but—"
>
> "It's a stupid name enough!" Humpty Dumpty interrupted impatiently. "What does it mean?"
>
> "*Must* a name mean something?" Alice asked doubtfully.
>
> "Of course it must," Humpty Dumpty said with a short laugh: "*my* name means the shape I am—and a good handsome shape it is, too. With a name like yours, you might be any shape, almost."
>
> **LEWIS CARROLL, *THROUGH THE LOOKING-GLASS***

IN EXPLAINING THE CHRISTIAN FAITH, we can begin almost anywhere, for Christianity relates to the whole of life—the outer world of natural science, the inner world of the human psyche, society at large, and individuals in particular. In short, we could begin with God, with people, or with the universe.

We will begin with something quite familiar to us—ourselves. What light does the Christian faith shed on us? Who are we? Or, more to the point, who am I? And, you who read this book: Who are you?

Christianity has an important—even startling—answer to this question. But before we can see just how startling and important we need to reflect. The question, who am I?, has lots of answers, one of the most interesting being your own name. As the first step in a long journey toward understanding the Christian faith, I would like you to join me in a look at what our names tell us about who we are.

LAST NAME FIRST

Take your own name, for instance. What does it tell you about yourself? First, look at your last name, your surname. If your family is Asian in origin, your first name may already be your last name, your surname. Where did you get it? From your father, of course. And he? Well, from his father. This indeed is your family name and represents the continuation of a long family line, a line extending—as amazing as it may seem—to the origins of the human race.

Of course, sometime in the distant past, if you trace your ancestry, you will find your family name disappearing from the records and the records themselves nonexistent. So, though you may soon lose track of your forebears, you are linked to the rest of the human race by biological heritage.

This linkage is just as certain through your mother's family as your father's, but the maternal line in the West, at least, is harder to trace. In any case, you are who you are because your father is your father and your mother is your mother. The offspring of any other pair would not be you.

Odd to think about, isn't it? Who would you be if your parents were different? Certainly not you.

Zen Buddhists ask a marvelously mind-wrenching question when they challenge young monks: What was your original face before your parents were born? Think about it. There is no answer. The question itself is nonsense, for you were not you before your biological origin. God may well have had you in mind—that we will con-sider later—but you did not exist. Each of us, in other words, is dependent on our parents for our very existence.

Moreover, none of us asked to be born. We exist by the will of others, and they by the will of others still, and some of us were never in-tended at all—at least not by our parents. We were "accidents."

What's in a name? How quickly our calm re-flection turns to shock! Our family name links us, for good or ill, to the family of man, to all its foibles, its accidents, its good intentions gone sour, its evil intentions turned good. Our very individual existence seems a matter almost out of anyone's control, even the control of the agents, our parents, who brought it into being.

It's a chancy thing, human life, especially our particular lives. Given slight changes of conditions in any of billions of situations down through the ages, I wouldn't exist, nor would you. But that's a might-have-been that isn't.

The fact is we do exist. Each of us is the product of a long line of hereditary characteristics, and each of us is the bearer of many more characteristics that we have the potential to pass on to our children. Our link to the past is permanent and unchanging. We cannot change our parents.

THE IMPORTANCE OF BEING SIRE

Actually, most of us do not want to change our heritage. Take the long and noble history of the Sire family, for instance! My wife and I once spent two fascinating (for me) days in eastern France, visiting one European branch of my father's family. Late in the nineteenth century my grandfather, Paul Louis Eugene Sire, emigrated from Neuchatel, Switzerland, and came to the United States. His father, Jacques Eugene, had left eastern France a generation before that and had established himself as a true Renaissance man by eventually becoming not only a watchmaker and taxidermist but also, so I was told, the curator of the museum in Neuchatel. At the age of eighty he was commissioned by the Swiss government to write a French grammar for their school system.

But by 1972 when I returned as the first of our side of the American family to do so, no Sire was left in Switzerland. Even in France only one small family still held the name: Robert Sire with four children, only two of them male. One of my sons has two boys; the other no children at all. The line is thin and close to extinction.

While in Blamont, France, a little village just a few miles from Switzerland, I saw the house Jacques Eugene's father built. Above the door the proof was etched in stone: C. Sire 1818.

Before Christopher Sire, all is lost in the mists of time. I am told, for example, that Sire is not our original name; that it used to be something like Esquire. But because my forebears were Huguenots (that is, French Protestants) and were subjected to severe persecution by Catholics, they changed their name. So maybe *Sire* does not really mean what it would seem to mean in French—*father*—but is short for some other, more dubious meaning.

I do know this. It became very clear while I was there that to be French and Protestant was good and to be German or Catholic was unspeakable. I never told my relatives that my wife's maiden name is Wanner, too obviously Teutonic. It surprised me, therefore, to be introduced while in eastern France to my fifth cousin—Jacques Schneller.

"Schneller!" I exclaimed. "But that's German."

After the shock of my insult had worn off, one of my relatives hastened to explain. "Oh no! Jacques is French. His brother is German."

Everything hangs on which side of the Rhine one lives on—the French or the German. Obviously, my cousin's brother (I guess he would be another cousin) lived on the German side. In the Alsace-Lorraine area, long fought over by the two countries, one's family name does not ensure one's nationality.

But family names are interesting. They reveal our origins; they testify to our roots in the past; they show that all of us belong on one continent. As John Donne said, "No man is an island."

I have long been interested in my father's side of the family. Perhaps that's because I loved my grandfather. He and grandmother—whom I really didn't like very much as a child—lived with our family for most of my childhood years.

So when I was shown the old family Bible in Christopher Sire's old house in Blamont, France, I lovingly copied the data on births and deaths recorded there.

Here I traced the joys and sorrows of Great Uncle Louis's family: Jules Henry (b. 28 Mar. 1870, d. 18 Apr. 1871); Georges Louis Alfred (b. 10 Jan. 1880, d. 18 May 1882); Louise Aline Emma (b. 28 Feb. 1883, d. an infant); Louis Alfred Pierre (b. 18 Sept. 1888, d. 12 Dec. 1916). Those are four of the ten children of Louis Sire (b. ?, d. 22 Jan. 1922). Four of them lived normally long lives. One died at the age of two, having fallen from the second floor of Christopher's house in Blamont. One, Louis Alfred Pierre, was a casualty of World War I.

I will spare you more details. My family line is interesting to me, not to you. But you, too, have a family tree. If you want to know yourself, you might wish to do some digging.

Ask your living relatives to tell their story of your family. Find out where you came from—the nationality, the ethnic origins in Europe, Asia, Africa, wherever. Does your family name have a meaning, such as Smith (from blacksmith) or Draper (from the weaving trade)? An internet search or books at your local library can help you get started on your exploration.

MIDDLE NAME SECOND

Now take your middle name. A few people in the English-speaking world have none; a few have two or even more. Where does your middle name come from? Not by necessity, but by choice—your parents' choice. So this, like your first name, is a given name. But you probably will find that it has also belonged to someone else among your near relatives. You were given this name because your parents wanted to honor someone they liked.

Take Walter. That's my middle name, but it's my father's first name. As far as I know, it was never used in the family before this. But it has been used again. It's the middle name of our second son—Richard Walter. The middle name of my first son is James. Look who got honored that time!

Of course, you may find that your middle name has been given to you for other reasons. Maybe it sounded nice when combined with your first name, like Ann with Mary. Or maybe it was just a beautiful name that your parents might have thought too odd to be a first name.

Maybe it was chosen for its meaning or its allusion to something good and beautiful in the past. Mary is the mother of Jesus. Elizabeth was her cousin and the mother of John the Baptist;

another Elizabeth was a great queen, and yet another a living queen.

If your middle name was chosen just for you, then it is a lot like your first name.

FIRST NAME LAST

Your first name (or middle and last name if you are Asian) is truly your given name. This is the one for you and you alone. If it honors a relative, be assured it is because your parents wanted you to be like him or her.

Our first son we named Eugene—not a very popular name for children in the United States—but one that honored my grandfather and my uncle, both of whom I grew up loving very much. I learned later that in the Sire family the name had been used at least once before.

Eugene to me is a beautiful name. Literally, it derives from Greek and means "well-born." How appropriate!

My own first name, James, doesn't fare so well. It's Hebrew, deriving from the same word as Jacob, and refers to the patriarch who cheated his brother Esau out of his birthright. The story is told in Genesis 25–27. When Jacob's character changed, God changed his name.

Literally James (or Jacob) means "the supplanter." Supplanter, indeed! Think of James the brother of Jesus, King James, Jamestown. How many Jameses do you know? In the early days of the United States it was among the ten most commonly used given names. Now how many Esaus do you know?

But again I want us to return to something important to you—your first name. Look up its meaning in a book such as George R. Stewart's *American Given Names* (see notes at the back). Ask your parents or closest relatives why you were given your name. Recently, some families in America are creating names based on their intrinsic beauty or ingenuity. If you are so blessed, then know that your parents really thought you special.

What your parents wanted for you may well be hidden in your given names. And what they wanted for you has influenced the way you have been raised. It's a key to the forces that have been deliberately shaping your life.

IN THE NICK OF TIME

Nicknames are a special case. How many do you have? Where did they come from?

The results of your reflection here are quite unpredictable, for nicknames can be terms of intimate endearment or vicious abuse.

The bulk of them, I suppose, fall somewhere in between. James is shortened to Jim or made diminutive in Jimmy. Martha becomes Marti; William becomes Bill; Marjorie becomes Marge or Marj or even Midge.

The intimacy of nicknames is one of their most valuable features. Only Uncle Don, Cousin Ken, and Ken's wife, Betty, call my wife Midge. Only my wife calls our son Richard by the name Cup or Cupcake.

Think of your nicknames. Are any of them special, limited to use by only one member of your family or one friend? This alone may make that person special to you or you to him or her.

But you probably have been branded with some nicknames you would rather forget. The kids in my elementary school called me Fim because, when I was learning to write script, I kept getting my Js backward. Much crueler are nicknames such as Fatty, Slim, Shorty, Stretch, Squint, Tub, and others that single out personal features we would rather weren't ours. We would never choose these names for ourselves, nor would our parents. Yet something about us or something nasty in the hearts of our school chums or work mates has triggered the appellation. And we are stuck with it—perhaps for life. Sometimes we outgrow our loathing of the name, and it becomes as acceptable to us as to our friends. We live it down by living with it.

One thing to notice, though: nicknames are ours alone. Like our first name they give us individuality. I was the only kid in our high school who was called Chemicals. My friends knew my first love was science, and I often gave them a hand with their homework.

BOXED IN BY NATURE AND NURTURE

What have we learned about ourselves from the study of our names? First, we note our firm grounding in the past. We are not on our own. We belong to our family, to our society. We are who we are not by our choice but by the will of others.

Did you have anything to say about where you were born? No. When you were born? No. Who your parents were? No. What society you were raised in? No.

None of us has had any control whatsoever over our genetic endowment. And yet that is fixed forever. It is beyond our control to modify it in any significant way. Biologically our nature is set.

Even our nurture has not been ours to control. I was born and raised in a ranching and farming community in northern Nebraska. By the time I came to consciousness, by the time it dawned on me that I was an "I" at all, much of my character and personality was fixed.

It's the same with each of us. By the time we ask that crucial question—who am I? Who is this specific, single, solitary individual?—it's too late for many changes to be made.

If we don't like the fact that we are American, or white, or short, or tone deaf, or artistically talented, we are out of luck. Stuck.

Our first name and nicknames tell us we are unique individuals. But that doesn't really satisfy our quest for human dignity. Any pebble on the beach is an individual, a unique individual. No two are identical. If we remain simply the combined product of nature and nurture, then there is nothing we can call our own. There is nothing that makes me anything more than nature's creation and culture's tool.

What, then, am I? Only an instrument wielded by forces beyond my control? That someone has named me, set me apart as an individual, may give me an illusion of identity, but it is only an imposed identity. It makes me only what others say I am.

Am I not also something on my own and for myself? Is all I do a product of external forces? Do I do nothing because "I" will to?

These are poignant questions. Worse, they have no good or satisfying answers if our analysis of who we are is limited to what we learn from reflection on our name. For that analysis finds us trapped in a box bounded on all sides by nature and nurture.

This indeed is our status if nothing of us transcends our physical-cultural existence. If our lives are ever to have value and meaning, if we are to have dignity as human beings, we must find a way out of this box.

That is precisely what the Christian view of human beings provides. Its answer to our dilemma is just as important and startling as I hinted it would be at the beginning of this chapter. We will see it unfold in the next.

QUESTIONS FOR REFLECTION

1. Consider your last name. From what nation and/or ethnic group does it derive? How long has your family (those from whom you derive) been living in the United States? Where did they come from? Does your last name have a literal meaning (e.g., Farmer, Smith)?

2. Consider your middle name. Why were you given this name? What does it mean?

3. Consider your first name. Why were you given this name? What does it mean?

4. List your nicknames and note how and why they were attached to you.

5. What have you learned about yourself from this analysis of your name?

6. Which do you think has played the largest role in your life: nature or nurture?

7. Read Psalm 139:1-18. What does this tell you about yourself?

CHAPTER TWO

Beginning with God

When I consider your heavens,
the work of your fingers,

the moon and the stars, which
you have set in place,

what is mankind that you are mindful of them,
human beings that you care for them?

PSALM 8:3-4

IMAGINE SHAKESPEARE'S GREAT CHARACTER Falstaff—a figure larger than life itself. What if, during the course of his action on stage, he were to have an identity crisis? Suddenly he doesn't know who he is. How will he find out? Who will provide the information?

First, he reflects on his name, but that doesn't help him much—Sir John Falstaff. Nobility, yes. But look at his friends, all rascals, except the prince. How noble can he be? *So who am I?* he asks.

Nowhere within the course of the play—its stage, its scenery, its other characters, the shape and substance of the dialogue—can Falstaff find out who he really is. The key piece of information is missing and, to him as a character, completely beyond his reach.

"You're a character in a play, my dear Falstaff," we might want to tell him. "You won't understand yourself until you understand your author. There he is, Shakespeare, over there behind that piece of scenery. Go talk to him."

We started our search for self-understanding by looking at our names. But like Falstaff we need to get beyond the stage on which our names give us our only meaning. We need to know the author of the play we are in.

That is just what the Bible gives us in the first lines of its first book. The Bible begins with God.

CREATOR AND CREATION

"In the beginning God . . ." are the opening words of Genesis, the book of beginnings. Nothing comes before him. He is the one who has always existed, who exists in himself and of himself and for himself. The theologians call this self-existence. God is the self-existent one, the only self-existent one, for there is but one God.

But God did not chose to remain alone. He chose to create: "In the beginning God created the heavens and the earth" (Genesis 1:1). Packed into this seemingly simple declarative sentence is the beginning of all our human quests for knowledge. For everything that exists either is in God himself or has been created by him. That is, at the heart of all we know are just two categories, which we can picture like this:

God

_____

Creation

Whatever is, is either one or the other.

This notion is of fundamental importance to our understanding because it means that nothing except God exists on its own. Nature does not; the universe does not; we as human beings do not. So we begin with a serious error if we think we can figure out who we are by starting with ourselves—the ability of our minds on their own to discern the true from the false. We are not autonomous as human beings. We are part of the created order. Whatever we are and do depends on God.

Genesis 1 goes on to detail some of the further acts of God in bringing creation into existence. He said, "Let there be light," and "there was light" (Genesis 1:3). He separated the light from the darkness, created and shaped the universe, formed the earth with its waters and its dry land, brought forth vegetation, ordered the motion of the heavenly bodies, created animals of many and various kinds, and then, finally, created the first people, Adam and Eve.

Genesis 2 pictures God fashioning Adam first, then placing him in the Garden of Eden "to work it and take care of it" (Genesis 2:15). And yet, while Adam is given control over the garden and may "freely eat" of its fruit, there is one important restriction. He is not to eat from "the tree of the knowledge of good and evil" (v. 17). In fact, if he does so, he will die.

Let us step back a moment from this account and ask what light it sheds on our concern in chapter one. There we found ourselves caught in the box bounded by nature and nurture. We seemed to find ourselves trapped within the confines of heredity and environment with no way to explain why we as individuals might be significant.

But when we turn to the Bible, are we any better off? According to what we have seen so far, the original pair of human beings, called our Grand Parents in John Milton's *Paradise Lost*, were caught in a box too—not the box of nature and nurture, but the box of divine will. Adam and Eve are who they are because they are created by God. They are trapped in God's box. They are like characters in an omnipotent author's play. Not only did God create them in a way pleasing to himself, but he also restricted their activity by imposing limits on what they may choose to do.

Perhaps the Bible does not solve the dilemma of human dignity but rather confirms our lowly status as puppets of the divine. But this conclusion is too hasty. We have left out of our discussion two factors that change the picture entirely. The first is the factor that differentiates human beings from all other parts of the created order. The second factor is the nature and character of God. We will have much to say about both in the remainder of this and in the following three chapters.

IN THE IMAGE OF GOD

After he had finished with the creation of the various animals, God turned his attention to the creation of human beings. It is important for us to see the way this is described in its entirety.

> Then God said, "Let us make mankind in our image, in our likeness, so that they may rule over the fish in the sea and the birds in the sky, over the livestock and all the wild animals, and over all the creatures that move along the ground."
>
> So God created mankind in his own image, in the image of God he created them; male and female he created them.

God blessed them and said to them, "Be fruitful and increase in number; fill the earth and subdue it. Rule over the fish in the sea and the birds in the sky and over every living creature that moves on the ground."

Then God said, "I give you every seed-bearing plant on the face of the whole earth and every tree that has fruit with seed in it. They will be yours for food. . . .

God saw all that he had made, and it was very good. And there was evening, and there was morning—the sixth day. (Genesis 1:26-29, 31)

This passage is packed with important information. But the most important for our purposes are the words that tell us just what makes a human being special, what sets a person apart from everything else in creation.

Human beings are made in God's image. Unlike all else in God's whole created order, human beings are made in his likeness.

It is true, of course, that all of the universe shows us something of God. "The heavens declare the glory of God;" says the psalmist, "the skies proclaim the work of his hands" (Psalm 19:1). But human beings do more. They bear the image of God himself. We can picture it like this:

God

Human beings

The rest of creation

Of course we are not to think of human beings as divine. But there is something about human beings that sets them apart from the rest of creation. We can summarize this by saying human beings are *created in the image of God*. That they are *created* sets them apart from God. That they are made *in God's image* puts them in special relationship to God and apart from the rest of creation.

In the immediate context, God's image is associated with two aspects of human nature. The first is the fact that human beings were born for intimate relationship with one another: "male and female he created them" (v. 27). No human being was made to be alone. This suggests that God himself is not alone. Later in the New Testament we realize this is true because God is triune—Father, Son, and Holy Ghost. There was, then, as Francis Schaeffer puts it, love and communication within the Trinity before God created human beings. We only reflect what already existed in God.

Second, human beings were given "dominion" over the rest of the created order—the animals and the plants—thus reflecting the ultimate dominion and sovereignty of God over creation. God has dominion by virtue of who he is in himself. Human beings have dominion because it was given to them by the Creator. We have been made "like" God in that respect.

Now we can begin to see why the box God puts us in is not one with constricted dimensions. We may not be who we are on our own, but look at whose image we bear! Being made in God's image means that human beings are not trapped by nature and nurture. We do not merely spout forth lines put in our mouths by a divine playwright. Each of us—male and female alike—is made in the image of God. Each of us is like the playwright himself. Our primary relationship is not to our parents or our society or even our Grand Parents, Adam and Eve. Our primary relationship is with God. Unlike Falstaff, we can in our own character love, obey, argue with, and rebel against the playwright.

If we are like God who is totally sovereign, if we have been given "dominion," perhaps we can break out of the mold of our family and culture, even the mold of our own names. Indeed this is the good news of the doctrine of creation. We have human dignity because we are made *in God's image*.

A DELICATE BALANCE

The balance, of course, is delicate. We are "great," but our greatness is endowed by another. We are over the rest of creation, but we are under God. We really exist, but our reality is created; its essential character is only an image of the really real.

That balance is beautifully captured by Psalm 8:

> LORD, our Lord,
>   how majestic is your name in all
>   the earth!
> You have set your glory
>   in the heavens.
> Through the praise of children and infants
>   you have established a stronghold
>   against your enemies,
>   to silence the foe and the avenger.
> When I consider your heavens,
>   the work of your fingers,
> the moon and the stars,
>   which you have set in place,
> what is mankind that you are mindful
>   of them,
>   human beings that you care for them?
> You have made them a little lower than
>   the angels
>   and crowned them with glory and honor.
> You made them rulers over the works of
>   your hands;

you put everything under their feet:
all flocks and herds,
    and the animals of the wild,
the birds in the sky,
    and the fish in the sea,
    all that swim the paths of the seas.
LORD, our Lord,
    how majestic is your name in all
    the earth!

The psalmist begins his reflection with God. God is so great, so majestic, his universe is so vast and awesome, what place is left for people? How can we be seen as significant in light of the tremendous power of God and the seemingly boundless extent of the heavens?

Then comes the astounding answer: "You have made them a little lower than the angels"! People have been crowned with "glory and honor" (Psalm 8:5) and given dominion over the works of God: flocks and herds, animals of the wild, and birds and fish.

And so the psalmist returns to praise God in the closing words as he has done in the opening ones: "LORD, our Lord, how majestic is your name in all the earth!" (v. 9). And note, too, that the psalmist recognizes God not just as the far-off Lord, but as our Lord, the one who deigns not only to create us in his image but to relate to us as the infinite-personal God in fellowship with the finite-personal people he has made especially like himself.

THE MAGNIFICENCE OF GOD

If the first factor preventing us from feeling boxed in is the notion that human beings are created in God's image, the second factor is to realize the magnificence of the God in whose image we are created.

If God were just an impersonal force, we would be machines. If God were like Zeus, constantly feuding as the chief God among many gods, we would be petty people of meager moral dimensions. It is commonly known that the heroes in the ancient Greek epics were far better than the gods. Lucky, we might say, not to have been created in their image! If God were like Shakespeare, we might be stuck with being Falstaff. If God were only austere and distant, we would have no hope for intimacy either with him or with each other.

If the God who made us were not himself in control of the entire creation, we would have no hope for breaking through the determination of nature and nurture, no hope for being in any sense our own persons. If God were not totally good, we would have no basis for thinking anything to be right or wrong. Anything would be morally permissible, and all hope for ethics would be gone.

But the God of the Bible is none of these. He is great and good, just and righteous, merciful and loving. Moreover, he is concerned for his whole creation and especially for those he made to be like himself.

But we are getting ahead of ourselves. The startling news that we are made in God's image must be followed by a much more detailed look at God himself. Only when we know God will we truly know ourselves.

QUESTIONS FOR REFLECTION

1. Read Genesis 1-2. How did the universe come into being? The plants? The animals?

2. How did people get here?

   What difference is there between human beings and the rest of creation, for example, the animals (Genesis 1:26-27)?

3. What does it mean to be made in the image of God?

4. Why do you suppose both male and female are mentioned in Genesis 1:27?

5. What kind of dominion were Adam and Eve given? (See also Psalm 8.)

6. What limits does this dominion seem to have?

7. Some scholars think that the word *dominion* is better translated as *stewardship*. What further limitations and implications does this suggest?

8. How does being made in the image of God solve the dilemma of the nature-nurture problem?

9. List some practical implications that being made in the image of God might have for you personally.

10. Meditate on Psalm 8 by reading it several times—at least until you can say with the psalmist, "LORD, our Lord, how majestic is your name in all the earth!"

CHAPTER THREE

A Name for God

> Moses said to God, "Suppose I go to the Israelites and say to them, 'The God of your fathers has sent me to you,' and they ask me, 'What is his name?' Then what shall I tell them?"
>
> God said to Moses, "I AM WHO I AM. This is what you are to say to the Israelites: 'I AM has sent me to you.'"

EXODUS 3:13-14

WHEN GOD CHOSE TO reveal himself to human beings, he did not do so all at once. As one New Testament writer put it, "God spoke to our ancestors through the prophets at many times and in various ways" (Hebrews 1:1). Some of the oldest recorded prophecy is found in the first five books of the Old Testament, traditionally attributed to Moses.

Moses stands in the forefront of Hebrew prophets not because God had not previously spoken with his people (for he had spoken, for example, to Abraham centuries earlier) but because it was to Moses that God entrusted the giving of the Ten Commandments and other more detailed laws that were to become the central authority for Hebrew life and thought. And Moses became the leader of God's chosen people, bringing them out of slavery in Egypt and on to the very edge of the promised land of Canaan.

How did Moses come to know so much about God and his ways? What can we learn about God through Moses' experience?

MOSES AND THE BURNING BUSH

First, we can see how God reveals himself to people in general. We can see, for example, that God speaks not just in abstract laws and philosophic generalities, but specifically and concretely to human beings in living situations. Then, through these human beings, God speaks to the rest of his people—you and me. In other words, we learn who God is not only by what he says to us through the prophets but also by how he spoke to them in their own life situation and in the context of specific places and specific times.

Moses did not suddenly emerge from his tent one morning with the entire message of God tucked neatly in his skull ready for delivery to the Hebrew people. God spoke to him in many different places and at many times. We will look at one of those times as Moses records it for us in the third chapter of Exodus.

The situation was this. Moses was in exile in the desert, a long way from the Hebrew people who were in slavery in Egypt. Many years had passed since he fled from punishment for slaying an Egyptian who had been beating a Hebrew. He was now tending the flock of his father-in-law in the land of Midian, somewhere east of Egypt, perhaps in the Sinai Peninsula.

Suddenly Moses saw a bush that was on fire but was not consumed. So he turned aside to see just what was going on. As he did so, a voice spoke to him from the bush: "'Moses! Moses!' And Moses said, 'Here I am'" (Exodus 3:4).

So far Moses was not aware that it was God who was speaking to him, but he didn't have long to wait. "Do not come any closer . . . Take off your sandals, for the place where you are standing is holy ground," the voice said. And then it gave its identity: "I am the God of your father, the God of Abraham, the God of Isaac and the God of Jacob." Moses knew what to do then. He "hid his face, because he was afraid to look at God" (vv. 5-6).

Already we can see some of the characteristics of God emerging from the events and the dialogue. God is a speaking God, one who chooses to communicate with people. He speaks their language, too, for Moses had no difficulty understanding what God said.

THE COMPASSION OF GOD

Moreover, God is one who takes the initiative. Moses was on a bypath of history, away from the family of God's people, and he would presumably have stayed there had God not arrested him from his daily task and set him off in a very different direction.

Additionally, God is holy. He is to be approached only with care and with reverence. His presence is awesome. He is not to be looked at face to face.

But God went on to say more about his concerns. He told Moses, "I have indeed seen the misery of my people in Egypt. I have heard them crying out because of their slave drivers, and I am concerned about their suffering. So I have come down to rescue them from the hand of the Egyptians and to bring them up out of that land into a good and spacious land, a land flowing with milk and honey" (Exodus 3:7-8).

The Lord went on to call to Moses to play a special role in his plan to save his people: "So now, go. I am sending you to Pharaoh to bring my people the Israelites out of Egypt" (v. 10).

So here we see God's compassion. He knows the hard lot of the Hebrews, and he is going to do something about it. He has a plan for their delivery. God, therefore, is a saving, delivering, liberating God. As the Lord of history—the Lord of human events—he is about to orchestrate a change in human affairs, national affairs.

To do this God chose Moses and gave him a particular role to play in the unfolding drama. Thus we see something of the way in which God relates to people. He does not, in a mechanical fashion, appear in some sort of UFO, descend to the sands of Egypt and ask the people to come aboard so they can be lifted to another place, another time, another dimension. Moses did not have a close encounter of the third kind. Rather, God spoke to him, honoring both him as a person and the children of Israel as a people.

We see that especially in the dialogue that ensued. Moses was not quite sure he wanted to be a part of God's plan. He replied, "Who am I that I should go to Pharaoh and bring the Israelites out of Egypt?" (v. 11).

Was Moses being humble? After all, he had been out of the center of action for a long time. Or was he frightened about the prospect? Surely to go back to Egypt would be dangerous. And who would believe him if he did go back?

How could any man do the job God was giving him?

Rather than upbraiding Moses for arguing with him, God simply said, "I will be with you." And he went on to give Moses a sign: "And this will be the sign to you that it is I who have sent you: When you have brought the people out of Egypt, you will worship God on this mountain" (v. 12).

God's presence with Moses was to be enough to ensure the success of God's plan. The sign itself would only be a sign when the action was complete! Till then Moses was to trust God and move out in obedience.

GOD'S NAME FOR HIMSELF

Again Moses had a question: "Suppose [notice that Moses does not say when] I go to the Israelites and say to them, 'The God of your fathers has sent me to you,' and they ask me, 'What is his name?' Then what shall I tell them?" (Exodus 3:13). Moses knew he would need some certification, as it were, to get the attention of the Hebrews. They would be wary of being misled by a false prophet.

God's reply is one of the great moments of revelation history. He said, "I AM WHO I AM. This is what you are to say to the Israelites: 'I AM has sent me to you'" (v. 14).

If we reflect back on the story, we can see that God had already identified himself as the God of Abraham, Isaac, and Jacob (v. 6). That name is, we might say, the name that ensured that Moses and the Israelites would not mistake him for one of the Egyptian gods or some other tribal deity. No, this was the God who had called Abraham out of Ur, who had loved Isaac and Jacob, and even cared for them by keeping them from starvation when a famine had come in the land of Israel.

By this name God shows us his character in relation to us as men and women. He is the God who does the sorts of things we already know about. God, in other words, ties himself to space and time. He is not ashamed to be the God of specific people, even though in their own lives they do not realize his greatness or live in total accord with his desires.

God's answer to Moses' question, however, takes us in a different direction. "I AM" is the translation of the Hebrew letters whose English equivalents are YHWH. In English Bibles this is often rendered Jehovah or Yahweh. The word comes from the Hebrew verb "to be" and indicates that God not only is but was and shall be. In short, God says, "I AM WHO I AM." He is the eternal God, the God not solely localized in time and space, not just the tribal God of Abraham, Isaac, and Jacob but the God of all, the Lord of the universe.

He is, as we saw in chapter two, the Creator. Always existing himself, he is the source of all else that exists. And he is what he is by virtue of himself and none other. He answers to no one, for he is the source of all answers.

NOT A GOD AMONG GODS

No wonder the people of Israel should listen to Moses! He represents the God who is Lord not only of the Hebrew people but also of Egypt.

Rabbi Monford Harris, former professor of Jewish texts and institutions at Spertus College in Chicago, once told me a story that derives from Hebrew tradition. The pharaoh, it seems, was troubled by hearing of this strange God of the Israelites. So he called his wise men together to ask them who this god was. They went back to their books and searched long and hard but could not find this god's name anywhere among the lists of gods. Rabbi Harris commented that, indeed, Yahweh is not a God to be listed along with other gods. He is I AM, not a god among gods but the one and only God. Even to think of him as a "god" is to blaspheme, for he is beyond all, above all, over all.

To be sure, the God of the Bible is just as Rabbi Harris has said. Yet he is also the God of Abraham, Isaac, and Jacob. He is the God of our history, and he involves himself in people's lives. He is not so distant as not to have been present with Moses in the burning bush and throughout his life, as he promised.

We know, too, from the New Testament that in Jesus Christ he has visited us in an even more intimate fashion. As the Word became flesh, he dwelt among us full of grace and truth (John 1:1-18).

The conversation between God and Moses continues through the remainder of Exodus 3 and spills over into Exodus 4. During the course of the dialogue God becomes angry with Moses because he continues to find reasons to disregard God's leading. But the upshot is that Moses sets off to follow God's call. We need not pursue the dialogue further. We have already learned enough to provide us a basis for understanding the nature and character of God. We will see much more of God's character in the following chapter.

QUESTIONS FOR REFLECTION

1. Read Exodus 2:23-3:22. Why was Moses in the desert? (See Exodus 2:11-22.)

2. Who initiates the encounter between God and Moses? How?

3. What is God's motivation for speaking with Moses? What does this tell us about God's character?

4. What does the fact that God speaks to people say about what kind of God he is?

5. How does God address Moses? What does this indicate about God?

6. What is God's first message to Moses? Why is it important that Moses learn this or be reminded of this? What is Moses' reaction? Why?

7. How does God first identify himself? Why is this an important matter for Moses (and us) to get straight?

8. How does God explain why he has come to Moses? What does this tell us about God's relation to human history? How does God act in relation to human events?

9. How does Moses react to God's plan for his life? Why could Moses get away with questioning God's call? What does God's reaction to Moses' objection say about God's attitude to the human personality?

10. How does God satisfy Moses' self-doubt?

11. What is Moses' second question? How does God respond? What does his name mean? Why should it answer Moses' need?

12. If you were asked, who is God? what could you answer based on this passage of Scripture? Summarize the characteristics of God that are revealed in this passage.

CHAPTER FOUR

The God Who Is

Immortal, invisible, God only wise,
In light inaccessible hid from our eyes,
Most blessed, most glorious, the Ancient of Days,
Almighty, victorious, Thy great Name we praise.

WALTER CHALMERS SMITH

THE PRIMARY TRUTH ABOUT GOD is that he is personal. Unlike the Hindu Brahman, the impersonal One who is beyond all duality and all distinction, the God of the Bible is a Person. And so it is as a person that he primarily relates to us.

God "heard" the groaning of the Israelites in Egypt, he "saw" their affliction, he "remembered" his "promise" to Moses' ancestors. He had compassion on his people. Then, when God wanted to move in the affairs of people, he got Moses' attention and addressed him directly: "Moses! Moses!" (Exodus 3:4). God called him by name and then spoke with him Person to person.

Yet, lest we think these personal traits put God solely on Moses' level, God's very next words were "Do not come any closer. . . . Take off your sandals, for the place where you are standing is holy ground" (v. 5). Thus God immediately emphasizes his holiness, his separateness from his creation.

We find, therefore, the same balance here as in Psalm 8. God is God, and thus he is majestic and infinitely powerful. Yet he has made us "a little lower than the angels" and crowned us with "glory and honor" (Psalm 8:5), and thus he can address us, call us by our name, and speak to us without crushing us.

The Bible has much more to say about God than what we find in Exodus 3. God has spoken to his people "at many times and in various ways" (Hebrews 1:1). In this chapter we will take a rather systematic approach to understanding God.

There are, of course, many ways to organize what the Bible tells us about him. Since God is infinite and inexhaustible, any scheme will ultimately prove inadequate. If we let it get in our way, it may even limit our vision, since we may tend to believe that somehow we have understood the depths of God by understanding something about a few of his attributes. But we will get nowhere without terms, categories, and some systematic way of seeing how the various attributes of God fit together.

The scheme I have chosen is simple. Since we have already seen God in action, as it were, relating personally to Moses and then to his people in Egypt, here we will look first at those aspects of God that relate primarily to his being (what he is in himself) and then at those attributes that relate to his character (what he shows himself to be in relation to us).

THE BEING OF GOD

The first truth about God's being is that he is self-existent. "The fool says in his heart, 'There is no God,'" the psalmist wrote (Psalm 14:1). But the wise person knows in his heart that just the opposite is true.

To Moses God identified himself as the I AM (Exodus 3:14). That is, God is in himself, of himself and for himself. The question, who made God?, once raised can only be answered one way. If someone made God, that someone would be God. Therefore, no one made God. He always was. God's self-existence, in other words, affirms his infinity. He is the Infinite in and beyond all time and space.

So, we go on to ask, Since God is, what is he like? What kind of being is he? Again one clear answer thunders from the Old Testament as God declares, "Hear, O Israel: The LORD our God, the LORD is one. Love the LORD your God with all your heart and with all your soul and with all your strength" (Deuteronomy 6:4-5).

The Lord is one—not a pantheon of gods. He alone is God, and therefore he alone is to be loved and obeyed. Notice how the very oneness of God is related by this command to human responsibility. And notice, too, that the proper human response is love. God is not some impersonal, intractable, distant force, but One to be loved. God's self-revelation never comes, therefore, in abstract, impersonal pronouncements, like some philosopher's rumination on the qualities of infinity. It always comes in the context of the personal, something to be grasped by all people and incorporated into their lives.

A further truth about God's being is hinted at in the Old Testament but does not become clear until the New. God's oneness is manifested in the Trinity: God the Father, God the Son, and God the Holy Spirit. The Trinity does not deny the monotheism of the Old Testament but is an unfolding of an aspect of God's being that was not yet revealed to Moses or David or even to such great prophets as Jeremiah or Isaiah.

When Jesus commissioned the disciples just before his ascension, he said, "Therefore go and make disciples of all nations, baptizing them in the name of the Father and of the Son and of the Holy Spirit" (Matthew 28:19). John spoke of the Word that was God (John 1:1) becoming flesh in

Jesus (John 1:14). And Jesus announced that the Counselor (the Holy Spirit) would come to the disciples and dwell in them after he himself had returned to the Father (John 14:16-17; 16:7-15).

The doctrine of the Trinity is, of course, a great mystery. How can God be One and yet Three? One way to express the relationship is to say, with theologian Geoffrey Bromiley, that "within the one essence of the Godhead we have to distinguish three 'persons' who are neither three gods on the one side, nor three parts or modes of God on the other, but coequally and coeternally God." Another way to say this is that the Father is God; the Son is God; the Holy Spirit is God. But, while each is God, none is strictly identical with any of the others.

We need not delve more fully into the mystery of the Trinity. It is sufficient here for us to note how the Trinity relates to love for God. In the Old Testament we are to love the One God; in the New Testament we see the nature of God in such profoundly personal terms in Jesus that love becomes an even more obvious response.

A fourth attribute of God's being is that he is spirit. When Jesus spoke with the woman at the well, he said, "God is spirit" (John 4:24). That is, God is not material. He is not limited to time and space. They are his creation, and while he relates to each person in time and space, he does not dwell in any one place, nor is his action limited in time.

It is interesting, therefore, that this revelation of God's nature should again come in a context involving human responsibility. The proposition "God is spirit" is immediately followed by, "and his worshipers must worship in the Spirit and in truth" (John 4:24).

THE THREE OMNIS

Next I want to mention a sort of trinity of attributes. I call them the three omnis—omnipotence, omniscience, and omnipresence.

God is *omnipotent*; that is, he is all powerful. Nothing is beyond the scope of his ability. Or better, he can do anything he wishes to do. As the psalmist says,

The LORD does whatever pleases him,
    in the heavens and on the earth,
    in the seas and all their depths.
    (Psalm 135:6)

And Jesus, noting the astonishment of his disciples when he explained how difficult salvation was for a rich man, commented, "With man this is impossible, but with God all things are possible" (Matthew 19:26).

We must, therefore, put away any notion that somehow God has lost control of things, that he must not be able to control his universe or the actions of people. God is omnipotent. Anything he wills to do he does. His omnipotence is simply his infinity expressed in terms of power.

God is also *omniscient*; that is, he is all knowing. John 1:1 associates God and the Word (*Logos*), which means total knowledge, wisdom, and reason. The psalmist puts it in intimately personal terms:

You have searched me, LORD,
　　and you know me.
You know when I sit and when I rise;
　　you perceive my thoughts from afar.
You discern my going out and my lying
　　　down;
　　you are familiar with all my ways.
Before a word is on my tongue
　　you, LORD, know it completely.
You hem me in behind and before,
　　and you lay your hand upon me.
Such knowledge is too wonderful for me,
　　too lofty for me to attain.
　　(Psalm 139:1-6)

God knows us inside and out. And why shouldn't he? He is our maker and the maker of our world. His omniscience is his infinity expressed in terms of knowledge.

Finally, God is *omnipresent*; that is, he is everywhere. We must be careful, here, not to think of God as being *in* nature in the sense of pantheism. God is not equated with his creation but is everywhere present to it. Again the psalmist gives a beautiful expression of this idea, revealing its personal dimension.

Where can I go from your Spirit?
　Where can I flee from your presence?
If I go up to the heavens, you are there;
　if I make my bed in the depths, you
　　are there.
If I rise on the wings of the dawn,
　if I settle on the far side of the sea,
even there your hand will guide me,
　your right hand will hold me fast.
If I say, "Surely the darkness will hide me
　and the light become night around me,"
even the darkness will not be dark to you;
　the night will shine like the day,
　for darkness is as light to you.
(Psalm 139:7-12)

God is with us regardless of where we are or even how much we try to escape him. His omnipresence is his infinity expressed in terms of locality.

The last attribute we will consider under the being of God is the fact that God is *Creator*. This is the first aspect of God mentioned by the Bible: "In the beginning God created the heavens and the earth" (Genesis 1:1). And the psalmist declares,

> He set the earth on its foundations;
>> it can never be moved.
> You covered it with the watery depths as
>>> with a garment;
>> the waters stood above the mountains.
> But at your rebuke the waters fled,
>> at the sound of your thunder they took
>>> to flight;
> they flowed over the mountains,
>> they went down into the valleys,
>> to the place you assigned for them.
> You set a boundary they cannot cross;
>> never again will they cover the earth.
>> (Psalm 104:5-9)

The psalmist goes on to extol God's majesty as Creator for twenty-six more magnificent verses. I will not quote them here, but would encourage you to read them in your own Bible. The psalm will make a fitting close to this section on the being of God.

THE CHARACTER OF GOD

Throughout this discussion on the *being* of God (what God is in himself) it has not been possible to avoid speaking also of the *character* of God (what he shows himself to be in relation to us). That is because God is so intrinsically personal that even his essentially unique attributes (those he holds as being who he is) relate to us as personal beings who are made in his image.

We turn now, however, to God's more obviously personal attributes—his righteousness, justice, compassion, mercy, and love. One passage of Scripture puts all these attributes together in one awesome self-revelation of God. Moses is on Mount Sinai where he has been commanded by God to come for further revelation. The book of Exodus records the event:

> Then the LORD came down in the cloud and stood there with him and proclaimed his name, the LORD. And he passed in front of Moses, proclaiming, "The LORD, the LORD, the compassionate and gracious God, slow to anger, abounding in love and faithfulness, maintaining love to thousands, and forgiving wickedness, rebellion and sin. Yet he does not leave the guilty unpunished; he punishes the children and their children for

the sin of the parents to the third and fourth generation." (Exodus 34:5-7)

In this very brief compass are contained the chief attributes of God's character. On the one hand, God is *merciful, gracious, slow to anger*, and *loving*. On the other hand, he is *just* and thus willing to let the consequences of human sin have their effect.

Both of these strains—the mercy of God and the righteousness of God—are wrapped up in the central aspect of God's character: his goodness. God is righteous and thus he can brook no evil. But he is also merciful, loving, and slow to anger. Therefore, he sees the affliction of his people in Egypt and comes to deliver them. They, of course, are sinful, and sin continues to have its effect in their lives, but God is with them to deliver them and lead them into the Promised Land.

In the New Testament we read of God's ultimate solution to the human dilemma of sin and our need for salvation. God became incarnate, the Word became flesh (John 1:14) and took up residence with his people. As we shall see later, it was ultimately through the death and resurrection of Jesus Christ, God the Son, that the seeming tension between justice and love is resolved. Only in the New Testament do we finally grasp how "righteousness and peace kiss each other" (Psalm 85:10).

THE PROPER STUDY OF MANKIND

This, then, is a glimpse of the God in whose image we are made. The more we learn about him, the more we learn about ourselves. Alexander Pope opened the second section of his essay "Essay on Man" with these lines:

Know then thyself; presume not God
　　to scan;
The proper study of mankind is man.

Nothing could be further from the truth, as we will see in the following chapter.

QUESTIONS FOR REFLECTION

1. We have noted in the previous study that the primary truth about God is that he is a person. From Exodus 3, summarize or list the various ways in which he shows himself as personal.

2. Each of the following verses indicates at least one of God's attributes. Next to the verse list that characteristic.

   - Exodus 3:14

   - Deuteronomy 6:4

   - Matthew 28:19

   - John 4:24

   - Psalm 135:6; Matthew 19:26

- Psalm 33:13-15; 139:1-6

- Psalm 139:7-10

- Genesis 1:1; Jeremiah 32:17

- Psalm 11:7; 145:17

- Leviticus 19:2; Isaiah 6:1–3; 57:15

- 1 John 4:7-16; Ephesians 2:4

3. What characteristics of God are mentioned in Exodus 34:6-7? What was Moses' response to this revelation?

4. In light of the attributes of God, what responses are appropriate for human beings?

CHAPTER FIVE

Man and Woman: The Image of God

It is dangerous to make man see too clearly his equality with the brutes without showing him his greatness. It is also dangerous to make him see his greatness too clearly, apart from his vileness. It is still more dangerous to leave him in ignorance of both. But it is very advantageous to show him both.

BLAISE PASCAL, *PENSÉES*

THE GOOD NEWS ABOUT GOD is who he is—his greatness, goodness, compassion, and love. The good news about ourselves as human beings is that God has made us like himself.

Before we explore the likeness between God and us, however, we must be careful to emphasize that comparisons can be developed in two ways. If we are only *like* God, if we are only in his image, then we are certainly not God and so we can emphasize the differences as well as the similarities. Indeed, we must emphasize the differences, or in our attempt to understand ourselves, we will make idols of ourselves. We will begin our analysis, therefore, with those aspects of God we seem least to reflect.

THE BEING OF HUMAN BEINGS

God is self-existent; we are *derivative*. God is the un-created; we are the created. "Let us make mankind," God said (Genesis 1:26), and God did so, not duplicating himself like a clone duplicates its "parent" but like an artist bringing into being something new and different from himself but bearing the characteristics of the artist in a profoundly personal way.

We are in his image; he is reality. If, therefore, we are to be truly who we really are, we will be like God. This simple but profound truth about ourselves is the key to a proper self-image. It both exalts us as important and significant—a special creation of God—and it puts us in our place below God, not equal with him or above him in being, honor, and dignity, but above all other creation. It is the healthy person who, short of proclaiming his own self-worth, looks to God as the origin of his life and seeks to become more like him in character.

God is One yet a Trinity; *we, as in his image, are also one in our personality and individuality, but are not complete without human community.* When Genesis tells us that God made us in his image, one of the first comments on what the word *image* means is "male and female he created them" (Genesis 1:27).

There are, in other words, two bounds on any given person's claim to human dignity. The first is that each person is God's creation and thus is not autonomous. The second is that each person is not complete without being in relationship to other people. To be fully human we must find ourselves and see ourselves as part of a larger whole. The marriage relationship is the deepest expression of this human community.

God's creation does not begin and end with each of us but with all of us. Our sense of humanness is not complete until we see ourselves in consort with our family, friends, community, country, and world. "From one man he made all the nations, that they should inhabit the whole earth," Paul told the Athenians (Acts 17:26). And unless we have at least a sense that we belong in the global community, we have stopped short of understanding what makes us who we are. As between the Persons of the Trinity, we need to see a balance between our individual selves as one and unique and our individual selves as part of a larger—much larger—whole.

God is Spirit; *we are spirit, soul, and body* (1 Thessalonians 5:23) or *soul and body* (Matthew 10:28). These are concepts I find difficult to handle. Some Christians have emphasized the threefold aspect of human beings and have drawn distinctions between a human being's body, soul, and spirit. Others have felt that the essential division is twofold: there is body on the one hand and there is soul (consisting of mind, emotions, and spirit) on the other hand. Still others, with whom I am most in sympathy, emphasize the unitary nature of human beings: a person is not a whole without the proper functioning of all her "parts," and all of these are extensions of or aspects of her central self. To be "spiritual," then, is to act, with all of who we are, in accordance with God's will.

We are unlike God in that we are created. That keeps us from being on a par with God in our being. But we are like God in such a way that we "have a spirit" or are "spiritual." Indeed, we are most spiritual when we are living and acting in accordance with God's revealed will and purpose for his people.

THE THREE NOT SO OMNIS

One thing is certain: no human being is omni-anything. We are limited.

Nonetheless, while God is omnipotent, *we are at least a little potent.* God's word to Adam and Eve at creation was that they "rule over the fish in the sea and the birds in the sky, over the livestock and all the wild animals, and over all the creatures that move along the ground" (Genesis 1:26).

In being given dominion, we were given the possibility of significant action in God's world. What we do counts. It matters to the world around us, for we can till the ground, cultivate the garden, and shape reality to human ends. God not only lets us do this; he even commands us to do so. This does not give us license to exploit the environment, ruining it for others (as some have charged Christian theology with doing). Rather, it makes us stewards of God's creation. We are to shape it to the glory of God and the benefit of ours and subsequent generations.

In dominion, we also have freedom—freedom to choose how to engage ourselves with the environment and, of course, with each other and with God himself. But that story comes later.

While God alone is omniscient, *we can know at least something.* It is in fact God's omniscience that grounds our capacity for knowledge. This is most fully expressed in the opening verses to the Gospel of John.

"In the beginning was the Word," John writes in John 1 (v. 1), thus proclaiming that meaning or intelligence is an aspect of God himself. God not only is; he is totally aware of who he is. He is a God of all meaning.

It is this God of meaning, this Word, who made the world itself: "Through him all things were made" (v. 3). Therefore, all of created reality has meaning. A God of meaning would not create absurdity. The world is indeed an orderly place shot through with meaningfulness.

But John goes on: "In him [the Word] was life, and that life was the light of all mankind" (v. 4). As people made in God's image, we bear the ability to grasp and comprehend something of the way in which God made the world. Moreover, John tells us, "The Word became flesh and made his dwelling among us" (v. 14). The result is that not only can we know something of creation, but also, "We have seen his glory, the glory of the one and only Son, who came from the Father, full of grace and truth" (v. 14).

Here, then, the great good news of creation is that there is a basis for our knowing. We do not just exist in a shadowy place where one person's opinion is as good as another's, where no one has any reason to think his thoughts are more than figments of his imagination. Truth is possible—for human beings as well as for God.

The third omni is omnipresence. Surely, here we are very unlike God. Well, not completely. If God can be said to be present throughout created reality, at all places and all times, *we are present in at least one place and one time.* God is self-existent; we are at least existent!

CREATOR AND SUB-CREATOR

God is Creator; *we are creative.* One aspect of human nature often overlooked in theological treatments is creativity. Sometimes, for example, it is said that only God is a creator. To be sure, God alone creates *ex nihilo,* bringing into being by his will things that are not. But it is also true that people bring new things into being from material already existing. In this they imitate (but do not duplicate) the creativity of God.

To be included in the works of human creativity are not only the fine arts but the crafts and sciences as well. For out of the creativity of people have come the new ideas and insights that mark the development of civilization and distinguish between the various cultures of the world.

To be human is to have the capacity to imagine new things and new ideas, to project this imagination forward onto the external world, shaping and fashioning that world after the patterns of our imagination. As God "imagined" and brought forth the world, so we imagine and bring forth tables and chairs, sculptures and symphonies, candles and computers.

THE CHARACTER OF HUMAN BEINGS

We now move from the attributes of God we least reflect to those which seem much more personally relevant. We could not be "human" without evidencing at least the rudiments of a sense of justice and righteousness and love. Yet it is here, too, that we now experience the greatest sense of alienation, for we know ourselves to be very poor reflectors of these attributes of God.

God is righteous. We can scarcely claim to be, and will see why in the next chapter. But, and this is an important qualification, our sense of righteousness persists even in our unrighteousness. We know that we *ought* to be better and to do better. *We have a capacity for moral reflection.*

This sense of *ought* is central to human nature and is in fact the reflection of God's righteous character. We retain the image of God in this way even though we recognize that the image is marred, our sense of the *ought* ill informed and off target. Still, our feelings of the injustices in the world attest to our retention of some God-likeness.

The same is true for love. While God loves perfectly, *we love sporadically, discriminately, wrongheadedly, and even illicitly.* As John says, "We love because he [Jesus] first loved us" (1 John 4:19).

But we do in fact love our children, our parents, our friends, and maybe some beyond our immediate family, and so there is still a vestige of the image of God left in us.

In Exodus 34:5-7, we saw that God is merciful, gracious, slow to anger, and forgiving. Likewise, inasmuch as we reflect these characteristics, we are evidencing the fact of our creation in the image of God.

Still, we see in all of these characteristics such imperfections in ourselves that we may wonder what happened to us. Surely, even if we were made in the image of God, we are not now bearing that image in perfection. What happened? Where did we go wrong? Is there any hope for restoring that image?

These are questions that will take us several chapters to answer even partially.

QUESTIONS FOR REFLECTION

1. Why is it important to recognize both the similarities and the differences between God and human beings?

2. In the space provided, list the "image" characteristic paralleling the "reality" of God. Biblical references should suggest the relevant characteristics.

The Nature of God	The Nature of Humanity
Self-existent (Genesis 1:26-27)	
One yet a Trinity (Genesis 1:27)	
Spirit (1 Thessalonians 5:23)	
Spirit (Matthew 10:28)	
Omnipotent (Genesis 1:26-30)	
Omniscient (Genesis 2:19-20)	
Omnipresent (Psalm 139:7-12)	
Creator (Genesis 2:19-20)	
Righteous (Genesis 2:15-17)	
Love (1 John 4:10)	

3. In what aspects of the above do we as human beings seem least able to reflect? Why?

4. From this analysis, frame a statement about the nature of the human dilemma.

CHAPTER SIX

The Bad News About Human Beings

> Here grows the cure of all, this fruit divine,
> Fair to the eye, inviting to the taste,
> Of virtue to make wise; what hinders, then,
> To reach, and feed at once both body and mind?
> So saying, her rash hand in evil hour
> Forth reaching to the fruit, she plucked, she ate;
> Earth felt the wound, and nature from her seat,
> Sighing through all her works, gave signs of woe
> That all was lost. Back to the thicket slunk
> The guilty Serpent.

JOHN MILTON, *PARADISE LOST*

AS WE SURVEY THE NATURE OF GOD and then examine the comparable characteristics of human beings, we get an odd feeling. Something doesn't fit. God is so great, so good, so just, so loving. He made the world good too. Throughout Genesis 1, as God finishes the various tasks of creation, he looks on his work and sees that it is good. Then when all of his creation is finished, Genesis records, "God saw all that he had made, and it was very good" (Genesis 1:31). But this does not describe our world as we know it.

Creation now seems scarred and broken. And God's special creation, the human race, seems worst off of all. It is not that everything has become totally corrupt but that it all seems cracked and marred. Try to find a perfect flower in a field of flowers. From a distance they all look beautiful; up close they are out of shape, worm eaten, wilted at one edge or another. Flower photographers will know what I mean.

With us as people, the flaws are even obvious from a distance. Our friends let us down, our parents are unreasonable, our children rebellious, our leaders out for their own power and glory. All humanity is at odds with itself.

Look inward at ourselves, and we see the conflict in our own hearts. We want to do good, at least sometimes, but we are unable to meet even our own standard of goodness. And often we don't even want to do or be what we know we ought to do or be. Our lives are a mixture of good and evil. Our world is a place where beauty and danger, as in the Kilauea Volcano, are often closely linked. The question is, How did things get so bent out of shape? If God's world, including humanity, was once "very good," what happened? Those questions are answered by the Bible in the account of the fall.

ONCE UPON A TIME . . . BUT NO LONGER

We live today in an abnormal world. Theologian Francis Schaeffer says we should remind ourselves of this daily as we try to understand and cope with the ordinary reality that now confronts us. It will help keep us from either romantic optimism on the one hand or existential despair on the other.

It is, as I have said before, part of the good news of creation that all of God's creation was once good. He made it that way because he himself is good. So at the foundational level we can affirm with certainty that God is good and his creation is good.

It is also true that creation, what once was so "very good," is no longer like it was. When God made Adam and Eve in his image, he endowed them with the capacity to imagine, to reason, to know, and to choose. This included the ability to choose apart from, indeed in opposition to, God himself.

The glory of being human included in it the possibility of disobedience, of acting out of accord with God who is good. In other words, it included the potential for evil. All of this is wrapped up in the command given to Adam seemingly immediately upon his creation: "You are free to eat from any tree in the garden; but you must not eat from the tree of the knowledge of good and evil, for when you eat from it you will certainly die" (Genesis 2:16-17).

This command, it would seem, was arbitrary. Was there anything wrong with the fruit of this tree? Was it not good? No, that won't square with God's own view of creation (Genesis 1:31). What then was the purpose of the command? Solely to stand as a mark of Adam and Eve's faithfulness to their Creator.

They could freely eat, according to their desires and their reason, of all other plants. This command alone marked their submission to God. This command, when obeyed, would show that the creatures made in God's image knew and continued to acknowledge that they were not independent, that they belonged to God. Image knew itself as image; it knew that its source was the only really real; that is, that its source was the ultimate reality.

Without such a command—one which could be freely obeyed or disobeyed—the climax of God's creation would not have reflected the goodness of God in freedom. It would have remained a mechanical, metaphysical goodness only, a goodness of being like the goodness of a tree or a lion or a lamb, but not a goodness existing with the possibility of evil. People would be computers without choice, programmed robots, amoral organic machines. They would not be in that sense like God; they would not be in his image.

If human beings are to be moral, they must have an opportunity to be immoral. On that hangs the tragedy of the human race. For in their freedom, Adam and Eve turned from God. Genesis 3 tells the story.

THE TEMPTATION

"Now the serpent was more crafty than any of the wild animals the LORD God had made," begins the writer of Genesis as he introduces the tempter (Genesis 3:1). Later in the Bible we learn who was really doing the tempting. The book of Revelation says, "The great dragon was hurled down—that ancient serpent called the devil, or Satan, who leads the whole world astray" (Revelation 12:9). There he is seen getting his just deserts.

By introducing Satan to the Garden of Eden, the Bible makes clear that there was nothing inherent in Adam and Eve that would make disobedience to God's command inevitable. The temptation came from outside, not from within. And what a subtle temptation it was!

"Did God really say, 'You must not eat from any tree in the garden'?" the serpent asks (Genesis 3:1). Thus he begins by casting doubt on God's Word to our first parents. Moreover, he gets the command wrong, and Eve has to correct him. No, she says in essence, "We may eat from all but one, and if we eat from that one, we will die." Eve clearly knows that one tree is forbidden, and she knows the consequences of disobedience.

But the serpent is not put off. He now directly challenges God's Word. "You will not die," he says. "Actually, God knows that you will be like himself if you eat the fruit." In short, he both accuses God of petty jealousy and appeals to the potential in Eve for imagining herself not only to be like God but also to be a god alongside God.

Eve, then, ponders the poisonous words of the serpent and concludes that the fruit of the tree is just what she wants: it is "good for food," it is "pleasing to the eye," it can give her "wisdom" (Genesis 3:6). Encapsulated here is the heart of all temptation—appeal to sensual desire (hedonism), to sensuous beauty (aestheticism), and to intellectual pride. All these are capped by the overriding impulse to spiritual pride, the desire to be God.

The essence of sin is pride—pride that expresses itself in rebellion against God. The image tells reality that it is no longer content with being the image but will settle for nothing less than being reality itself.

In so doing, of course, the image of reality is itself shattered. Human beings are created. They depend for their existence on God. To say and act otherwise is to believe the lie of Satan, the Big Lie. And when that happens, the consequences are inevitable. If human beings will not be who they really are, they must become less than they are.

THE FALL

Eve ate the fruit. She gave some to Adam and he ate it. And then both of them suddenly realized that they stood exposed before God. Their eyes were opened and they "realized they were naked" (Genesis 3:7).

Adam and Eve knew good and evil before because God had told them about obedience and the consequences of disobedience. They had an intellectual—and quite adequate, we must add—knowledge of good and evil. Now they knew good and evil by becoming evil.

We can picture it like this. All of us know what a widow or widower is. But only a few know it by being one. Adam and Eve came to know evil by experience. They experienced evil by becoming evil.

Thus they were guilty. They had true moral guilt before God. And they felt it. They knew God would be displeased. Their only hope, they thought, was to hide. And so they covered their nakedness and they slunk back into the trees when God came to speak with them again.

But no one can hide from the omniscient God. And when God confronts them, we see how the fruit of the tree has affected them. We have a hard time imagining the unfallen human pair. What would it be like to be truly in God's image? We have no difficulty recognizing the fallen human pair. They are just like our parents. No, they're just like us.

"What happened to you?" the Lord God says. "Did you eat the fruit I told you not to eat?"

Without hesitating Adam sidesteps the question. Denying his own responsibility, he says, "The woman *you gave me* gave me the fruit to eat." According to Adam, two others are responsible—Eve and God himself!

Eve likewise refuses to take responsibility, casting it on the serpent. "He tricked me," she says.

THE CONSEQUENCES

Then the consequences of Adam and Eve's action come down in full force as God proclaims the results to the serpent, to Eve, and to Adam. The serpent will from now on be the lowest of the beasts. And though the serpent, seen as representing Satan, shall trouble the human race, he shall eventually be crushed by the "seed" of Eve. Here is a hint of the triumph of Christ over Satan, worked out on the cross and consummated at the end of time.

Eve will bear children in pain and find herself ruled by Adam; thus the fall sets up the conditions for the oppression of women.

Adam will have to work hard to control the growth of thorns and thistles. Work itself is not seen as a curse, for before the fall Adam was commanded to till the ground and take dominion over the animal kingdom as well. But now his task will be much more difficult. "By the sweat of your brow / you will eat your food," God says (Genesis 3:19).

Spiritual death—the separation of mankind from God—had already set in, for Adam and Eve were now estranged, alienated personally from God. Now they hear the curse of physical death as well, for Adam (and Eve too) will return "to dust" (v. 19). Physical death, as was promised, will eventually be their lot.

A HINT OF HOPE

Before he casts them from the Garden of Eden, God does one more thing that hints at what he will be doing throughout the history of our sojourn here on earth. He makes "garments of skin" (Genesis 3:21) and clothes them, thus symbolizing in the killing of the animals, some theologians say, the sacrifice of Jesus on the cross.

From here on the story of humanity is a variegated narrative of trial and tragedy. Cain kills Abel. The world becomes populated and then so corrupt God eliminates all but a handful by a flood. Abraham becomes God's choice as the founder of a new family of God's people. But things go badly there too.

Prototypes of God's ultimate solution to the human dilemma abound in the Old Testament accounts. Finally, in the fullness of time, God sends his Son to show us what it really means to bear God's image and then to die for us, thus making peace for us with God, with each other, and with ourselves. But we are getting ahead of ourselves. We will pick up the threads of the story of mankind in the chapter following the next one.

QUESTIONS FOR REFLECTION

1. When God finished with his creation, what was his attitude toward it? (Genesis 1:31; see also verses 4, 10, 12, 18, 21, 25.)

   Read Genesis 2:15-17 and 3:1-24. What were Adam and Eve to do in the garden (2:15)? What were they not to do (2:17)?

2. What would happen if they did what they were commanded not to? Did they know this (Genesis 2:17)? Did they obey God?

3. What tempted Eve (Genesis 3:4-6)? What tempted Adam? What does this reveal about Adam and Eve, that is, the character of each of them?

4. What, in one word (or two or three), was Adam and Eve's sin?

5. What was the first result of their disobedience (Genesis 3:7)? Why did Adam and Eve hide from God?

6. How did Adam explain his sin to God? How did Eve explain her sin to God? Are these good explanations? Why?

7. List the results of the sin to each of the following (Genesis 3:14-22): the serpent, the man, the woman, earth, and mankind.

8. What provision did God make for Adam and Eve (Genesis 3:21)?

9. Why did God cast them from the garden?

10. The Westminster Shorter Catechism asks, "What is the chief end of man?" And it answers, "Man's chief end is to glorify God, and enjoy him for ever." How did Adam and Eve keep that purpose from being realized?

11. Would you say that now creation—all of it, man, woman, animals, nature, planets—is good? What is the world we live in like now? How did the world get into its present shape?

CHAPTER SEVEN

Sin: From the Inside Out

What a chimera then is man! What a novelty! What a monster, what a chaos, what a contradiction, what a prodigy! Judge of all things, imbecile worm of the earth; depository of truth, a sink of uncertainty and error; the pride and refuse of the universe! Who will unravel this tangle? . . .

Know then, proud man, what a paradox you are to yourself. Humble yourself, weak reason; be silent, foolish nature; learn that man infinitely transcends man, and learn from your Master your true condition, of which you are ignorant. Hear God.

BLAISE PASCAL, *PENSÉES*

THE STORY OF ADAM AND EVE is not only an account of something that happened long ago and far away. It is the story of each of us. For when the first human pair disobeyed God and God put them out of the Garden of Eden, the whole of the human race was separated from intimate contact with their Creator. No longer could Adam and Eve converse quietly, freely, and easily with God.

And, apart from God's work in Christ on the cross, no longer can we do this today.

When we read Genesis 3, we are struck with its relevance to us. It is our story too. The apostle Paul tells us that the sin of Adam and Eve affected the whole human race: "In Adam all die" (1 Corinthians 15:22). But we hardly need to be told this, because by the time we are old enough to understand such a notion, each of us has recapitulated the fall in our own lives. As children we soon begin to assert ourselves against our parents; by the time we know what we are doing, we are caught in a pattern of rebellion and self-assertion that continues to characterize our life on earth. In the old Puritan catch phrase, "In Adam's fall we sinned all."

In this chapter we will look more closely at the nature of sin, the nature of the human dilemma.

THE NAMES OF SIN

Surveying the various words the Bible uses to label sin, theologian John Murray says, "Sin is failure, error, iniquity, transgression, trespass, lawlessness, unrighteousness. It is unmitigated evil." The apostle John writes, "Everyone who sins breaks the law; in fact, sin is lawlessness" (1 John 3:4). Murray, commenting on this verse, writes, "Law is the transcript of God's perfection;

it is His holiness coming to expression for the regulation of thought and action consonant with that perfection. Transgression is violation of that which God's glory demands of us and is, therefore, in its essence the contradiction of God." Then, to indicate that people who sin are well aware that this is what they are doing, the apostle James says, "If anyone, then, knows the good they ought to do and doesn't do it, it is sin for them" (James 4:17).

Two passages of Scripture bear special relevance to our understanding of sin. We will, therefore, deal with them in some detail. The first is James 2:8-11:

> If you really keep the royal law found in Scripture, "Love your neighbor as yourself," you are doing right. But if you show favoritism, you sin and are convicted by the law as lawbreakers. For whoever keeps the whole law and yet stumbles at just one point is guilty of breaking all of it. For he who said, "You shall not commit adultery," also said, "You shall not murder." If you do not commit adultery but do commit murder, you have become a lawbreaker.

James makes a striking statement here: whoever breaks one commandment is guilty of breaking all of them! Surely, this sounds odd. How can that be? It doesn't sound fair.

But James gives the reason—an explanation that gets to the root of the nature of sin. He says that the reason breaking one law is like breaking all of them is that *God* gave the law. It is not breaking a rule that is important, but violating a relationship. In the law God has expressed to us what it means to be good and to act justly and righteously. If we refuse to obey him on one point, we have refused *him*. It is he who is important.

A right relationship to God is the center of morality, the basis of ethics. When we violate one law, we become in his sight (and in reality) a "lawbreaker," a "transgressor," one who has stepped over the line of proper action. As Murray puts it, "The most characteristic feature of sin in all its aspects is that it is directed against God." If we have violated our relationship with God, if image tells reality that image is reality, it has ceased to be what it really is. We are then lawbreakers, transgressors, and must be treated as such.

THE PROBLEM WITHIN

The second passage of Scripture is Mark 7:1-23. Here Jesus is challenged by the Pharisees and scribes who complain that Jesus' disciples are breaking the "tradition of the elders." They were eating without going through the prescribed ritual of washing their hands.

Jesus is quick to respond. He calls them hypocrites and quotes a strong rebuke from Isaiah:

> These people honor me with their lips,
>> but their hearts are far from me.
> They worship me in vain;
>> their teachings are merely human rules.
> (Mark 7:6-7, quoting Isaiah 29:13)

Jesus says, "You have let go of the commands of God and are holding on to human traditions" (Mark 7:8). Then he gives a specific illustration of how their own "tradition of the elders" violates the direct commandment of God by giving them a way to get out of responsibility for elderly parents.

Finally, Jesus draws his conclusion: "Nothing outside a person can defile them by going into them. Rather, it is what comes out of a person that defiles them" (v. 15). When his disciples ask him for a further explanation, he says,

> Don't you see that nothing that enters a person from the outside can defile them? For it doesn't go into their heart but into their stomach, and then out of the body. . . . What comes out of a person is what defiles them. For it is from within, out of a person's

heart, that evil thoughts come—sexual immorality, theft, murder, adultery, greed, malice, deceit, lewdness, envy, slander, arrogance and folly. All these evils come from inside and defile a person. (vv.18-23)

Sin is a condition of the heart, an internal state, a fountain from which flows poisonous muddy water. We are not sinners or lawbreakers because we sin and break the law. Rather we sin and break the law because we are sinners and lawbreakers.

Our problem is that we exist in a state of rebellion—rebellion against God that leads us into rebellion against others and even a brokenness of our inner selves so that we conduct an inner fight as well.

Notice the "sins" that Jesus lists. Some are those we might consider major: theft, murder, wickedness, deceit. Some we might consider minor: evil thoughts, coveting, envy, pride, licentiousness, and foolishness. A couple of sins are so common today that some may not think them sinful at all: fornication and adultery. Some are external: theft, murder, and adultery. Others are internal: evil thoughts, envy, and pride.

But all of them come out of the heart, out of the central core of our personality. As Jeremiah said,

The heart is deceitful above all things
and beyond cure.
Who can understand it?
(Jeremiah 17:9)

So the problem we face as human beings could not be more desperate. We are sinful from the inside out. If we are to become like God again, if his image is to be restored in us, it will have to be from the inside out.

PORTRAIT OF A SINNER

But surely, we may ask, doesn't God know our plight? Can't he see our situation, and, knowing our finiteness and weakness, simply accept us anyway? Why make so much fuss about a problem we can't seem to do anything about?

The answer to those questions takes us back to the character of God. God is just and righteous. If he merely patted us sinners on the back and said, "There, there. I understand. It's okay," he would do violence to his own righteousness. Moreover, he would not be honoring his own choice to give his special creation freedom to be like himself. We chose not to be like him. He leaves us responsible for our choice. As to his attitude toward what we have done with that choice, we are not left in doubt.

The apostle Paul, quoting several passages from the Old Testament, says,

"There is no one righteous, not even one;
　　there is no one who understands;
　　there is no one who seeks God.
All have turned away,
　　they have together become worthless;
there is no one who does good,
　　not even one." (Romans 3:10-12)

Sin is universal. There is no person in the world whose heart does not spew forth sinful thoughts and actions. Paul traces the sinfulness to its results in the whole body—throat, tongue, lips, mouth, feet, eyes:

"Their throats are open graves;
　　their tongues practice deceit."
"The poison of vipers is on their lips."
　　"Their mouths are full of cursing and
　　　　bitterness."
"Their feet are swift to shed blood;
　　ruin and misery mark their ways,
and the way of peace they do not know."
　　"There is no fear of God before their
　　　　eyes." (Romans 3:13-18)

Do you get the picture? Can you see that you and I and all people are like this? Do we realize that the venom of snakes is under our lips? Ghastly thought! That our throats are open graves? Gruesome! Such is the language that must be used if we are to see ourselves as God sees us.

What is worse, God holds us responsible for our sinful condition. After pointing out how corrupt and deceitful we are, Jeremiah records the words of God:

"I the Lord search the heart
     and examine the mind,
to reward each person according to their
          conduct,
     according to what their deeds deserve."
(Jeremiah 17:10)

The apostle Paul clarifies this for us when he writes, "The wrath of God is being revealed from heaven against all the godlessness and wickedness of people, who suppress the truth by their wickedness" (Romans 1:18). And elsewhere he says, "The wages of sin is death" (Romans 6:23). Fortunately, there is more to that verse, but here I wish only to bring home with force the desperate condition all of us are in. "The wrath of God is . . . a reality," Murray comments, "and the language and teaching of Scripture are calculated to impress upon us the severity by which it is characterized."

Is there a way out of this dilemma? Is the image of God in us so far from reality that there is no hope for recovery? Is the good news of creation obliterated by the bad news of sin? Is the story of humanity a tragedy?

Thanks be to God, no. The story of how God deals with the problem of human rebellion will be the subject of the next three chapters.

QUESTIONS FOR REFLECTION

1. How do the following verses define sin: 1 John 3:4, James 4:11, and James 2:8-11?

2. How serious is breaking even one of God's laws? Why? (James 2:10-11)

3. Read Mark 7:1-23. List the people who were present during this event. What role did each play?

4. What issue did the Pharisees raise?

5. What was Jesus' response?

6. Concerning the money given to God (Mark 7:11), R. Alan Cole writes, "At the very heart of the law, filial piety was enshrined: but by a typically rabbinic twist of values it was possible to vow to the Temple all the money that would normally have been expended on the maintenance of parents, and so to avoid

the plain demands of duty, obvious enough to the pagan outside." What point does Jesus make regarding this?

7. Where does sin originate, according to Jesus?

8. What sins does Jesus list? What do they mean?

9. What is the difference between sin and sins?

10. Summarize your analysis of Mark 7 by defining sin as it is used in this passage.

11. Read Romans 3:9-20. How many people are captured (bound, under the power of) sin? How many are going to be held accountable to God?

12. How does Paul describe those in this situation? Do you seem to be this bad off? Why?

13. Read Romans 1:18 and 6:23. What are the ultimate results of sin?

14. Reflect on what the Scriptures you have studied here tell you about yourself.

CHAPTER EIGHT

God in Search of His People

> History . . . is the shape, the meaning of events. It is the direction, the gist, of things that happen in high times at real places. . . . It is not the making of a point, but the catching of a point; not the assignment of meaning, but the discovery of meaning; not the fabrication of legends about a mythical beast, but the snarling of a real one. History . . . *is* the beast. What men have had to say about it is only the joyful or desperate record of the chase.

ROBERT FARRAR CAPON, *AN OFFERING OF UNCLES*

SOME OF THE MOST poignant lines any poet ever penned are those of John Milton at the close of *Paradise Lost*. The scene is the expulsion of Adam and Eve from the Garden of Eden. Having eaten the forbidden fruit, they must now suffer the consequences of their action—separation from intimate fellowship with God.

> Some natural tears they dropped, but wiped them soon;

The world was all before them, where to
          choose
Their place of rest, and providence their
          guide;
They hand in hand with wandering steps
          and slow,
Through Eden took their solitary way.
          (XII, 645-49)

There is an intended note of ambiguity here. As
they leave the Garden, they are both solitary (the
only couple) and communal (hand in hand). They
are both under Providence (the superintending care
of God but not his close face-to-face presence) and
they and their progeny—us—are on their own to
choose for themselves how they will search for rest.

This dual, ambiguous situation is the backdrop
for God's relationship with humankind from Eden
till the end times when God's people are totally
transformed as the bride of Christ and become
citizens of the New Jerusalem envisioned in Revelation 21. People do have their own way. And
the story of mankind is an ugly account of murder,
treachery, war, lust, and corruption. Yet God does
not totally abandon his creation. Though the
image they bear of God is distorted, though they
do not deserve anything but judgment, he refuses to let sin frustrate his love for those he fash-
ioned especially for close relationship with him.

The Bible is the record of this dual relationship: humanity going full tilt toward total separation from God and God breaking into this historical causal nexus, searching for his people, wooing them back to him. We will now examine the high points of this story of God's search.

ABRAHAM: THE FATHER OF A GREAT NATION

We have already noted in chapter six that God by clothing Adam and Eve began then to show his concern for his people. We also noted that soon after their expulsion from Eden one of their children murdered the other. In subsequent generations the growing family of mankind turned its back so totally on God that he destroyed all but Noah and his family through a flood. The events in the early history of man, however, are shrouded in obscurity. We know neither time nor place with any assurance.

When the Bible turns to Abraham, however, both time and place come into focus. We come to learn the story of mankind through the story of Abraham, his children, and his children's children; that is, through the Hebrew people. Yet, as we shall see, it is not the story of one people only; it is a universal story. The beginning is set about 2000 BC in Ur of the Chaldees, a city on the Persian Gulf in present-day Iraq. As with Moses in the wilderness, the initiative comes from God.

The Lord had said to Abram, "Go from your country, your people and your father's household to the land I will show you.

"I will make you into a great nation,
   and I will bless you;
I will make your name great,
   and you will be a blessing.
I will bless those who bless you,
   and whoever curses you I will curse;
and all peoples on earth
   will be blessed through you."
   (Genesis 12:1-3)

When God revealed himself to us, he chose a particular man in a particular place. From this man flowed a particular people—the nation of Israel, the Hebrew people. But through this man and this people, all persons everywhere, every man and every woman, every nation and every people, may be blessed. The issue will be how they relate to Abraham and to the revelation of God that comes through him and subsequent prophets of Israel.

Abraham followed God's leading from Ur up the fertile crescent and down into Palestine. When Abraham and his wife were very old, they finally had a son, Isaac. God tested Abraham's faith by asking Abraham to offer Isaac as a sacrifice and then, just in time, providing a ram as a substitute for Isaac. This story serves as a further hint of how God will solve the problem of human sin. God will send his own Son as a sacrifice, substituting his Son for us who deserve, as children of Adam, the penalty of death.

Isaac's family consisted of two sons, Jacob and Esau. From Esau came the Semitic tribes now called Arabs. From Jacob came the Jews (the twelve patriarchs who father the twelve Israelite tribes). Before these twelve families could grow, however, a famine struck the land of Canaan (about 1700 BC) and Jacob took his family into Egypt where they received food, but were eventually enslaved.

MOSES: THE LIBERATION, THE LAW, THE SACRIFICE, THE MESSIAH

The biblical account then picks up again with the Hebrew people, now several million in number, groaning under slavery in Egypt. Though Moses had fled into Sinai after killing an Egyptian, God chose him—as we saw in chapter three—to lead his people out from Egypt. The exodus becomes in later biblical thought a symbol and demonstration of God's interest in delivering poor and oppressed humanity from their bondage in sin.

While the Israelites were in Sinai on their way to the Promised Land of Canaan, they received from God through Moses the Ten Commandments and an elaborate civil and ceremonial law. These formed the basis for the peculiarly Jewish contribution to culture, setting apart the Hebrew people from all other tribes and nations. Since they were to be the specific vehicle of God's revelation of himself to all humanity, this was a vital necessity.

We are all familiar with the Ten Commandments. In the modern world they are still recognized as normative for traditional morality. The ceremonial law, however, deserves some comment, for, like the averted sacrifice of Isaac, it pictures God's way of dealing with sin.

The sacrificial system is quite elaborate, making different demands for different sins. One of these sacrifices, however, is especially significant (Leviticus 16). On the Day of Atonement, Aaron, the chief priest, was not only to sacrifice a bull as a sin offering for himself (for he, too, was a sinner) but also he was to sacrifice two goats. The first he was to kill as a sin offering for the people, thus symbolizing that the wages of sin (death) was being transferred to the substitute goat. The second goat remained alive. Aaron was to place his hands on the head of this goat, confess over him the sins of the people, and thus transfer these sins to the animal. The goat was then sent into the wilderness, symbolizing the fact that God takes away the sins of his people, as a psalmist later proclaimed: "As far as the east is from the west, / so far has he removed our transgressions from us" (Psalm 103:12).

It is to Moses, too, that God first proclaimed the coming of one who would be a special prophet (Deuteronomy 18:15-19). Throughout the Old Testament period, subsequent prophets added to this hope for a Messiah who would lead God's people and save them from destruction.

A tragic pattern emerged while the Hebrew people were in the wilderness. Over and over again this cycle was repeated. While things went well with them, they would forget God and begin to break his laws. God would see this and bring judgment. The people would recognize their sin and repent. God would bring prosperity. And the cycle would repeat.

It is, in fact, because of this kind of behavior that the Israelites had to spend forty years in the desert. Only two people, out of all those who left Egypt, lived to enter the Promised Land—Joshua and Caleb. Even Moses was allowed only a glimpse from a high peak.

THE CONQUEST AND THE TWO KINGDOMS

The conquest of Palestine was led by Joshua in the thirteenth century BC. After the land was taken and divided into twelve sections, one for each of the twelve tribes, the people lived under a loose federation. For a period of about two hundred years "judges" were chosen by God to keep this rather chaotic situation in control. Finally, under pressure from surrounding non-Jewish tribes, the people sought God for a king. Saul was selected first. Then came David, the greatest king of all, one whom the New Testament sees as a type of Christ.

David, Saul's successor, consolidated into a single nation the territory held by the tribes. Never before nor ever since were Israel's borders as extensive as during his reign. It was during the period of the single monarchy that much of the Wisdom Literature (the Psalms and Proverbs) was written.

King Solomon, David's son, capped off the expansion of the nation by erecting a magnificent temple, thus bringing the worship of all Israel to a single, central location.

After the death of Solomon, the nation divided in two: a northern kingdom called Israel with its center in Samaria and a southern kingdom called Judah with its center in Jerusalem. Both kingdoms were beset by the superpowers of that era—Assyria and Babylon to the north and east and Egypt to the south. In 722 BC the northern kingdom fell to Assyria. In 586 BC Jerusalem and the southern kingdom fell to Babylon and all of the able-bodied Hebrews were carted into exile. Israel's existence as a nation with self-determination was at an end. Not until 1948 was it again to have an independent political existence.

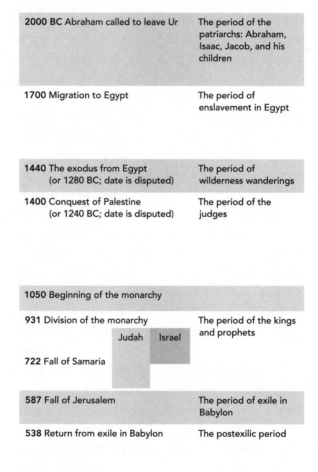

2000 BC Abraham called to leave Ur	The period of the patriarchs: Abraham, Isaac, Jacob, and his children
1700 Migration to Egypt	The period of enslavement in Egypt
1440 The exodus from Egypt (or 1280 BC; date is disputed)	The period of wilderness wanderings
1400 Conquest of Palestine (or 1240 BC; date is disputed)	The period of the judges
1050 Beginning of the monarchy	
931 Division of the monarchy	The period of the kings and prophets
Judah Israel	
722 Fall of Samaria	
587 Fall of Jerusalem	The period of exile in Babylon
538 Return from exile in Babylon	The postexilic period

Figure 8.1. Timeline of the history of Israel

THE MESSAGE OF THE PROPHETS

The Bible, however, does not just recount the facts of Israel's political life. Through the prophets God spoke almost continuously in some form or other to his people. The basic message was always the same. In his words to King Solomon: "If my people, who are called by my name, will humble themselves and pray and seek my face and turn from their wicked ways, then I will hear from heaven, and I will forgive their sin and heal their land" (2 Chronicles 7:14). If they continued in their wicked ways, God's protective hand would be removed and destruction would come.

It is clear from the prophets that the people's sin included violation of all manner of God's Law. They sinned against God through idolatry and false religion, and against each other through economic oppression, lying, adultery, theft, coveting, and the like. Throughout the centuries from the first king to the last independent city— Jerusalem—there were occasional revivals. King Josiah led a major one in the decades just before the fall of Jerusalem. But what repentance there was was not accompanied by reformation, and God let his people be led away once again into captivity.

Unlike the Jews in Egypt, however, the Jews in Babylon prospered. Then some seventy years later they returned to Jerusalem, rebuilt the totally devastated city, and constructed a new temple, one not nearly so imposing as Solomon's.

THE NEW COVENANT: ALREADY BUT NOT YET

During the final days in Jerusalem and also during the exile, the prophets Jeremiah and Ezekiel saw that God was preparing a new way of relating to his people. No longer would God be tying himself strictly to a nation or a single people. He would establish a new covenant. Though it would be with the house of Israel and Judah, it would directly involve the people themselves rather than be mediated through the religious system of Judaism:

> "This is the covenant I will make with the
>   people of Israel
>   after that time," declares the LORD.
> "I will put my law in their minds
>   and write it on their hearts.
> I will be their God,
>   and they will be my people.
> No longer will they teach their neighbor,
>   or say to one another, 'Know the LORD,'
> because they will all know me,
>   from the least of them to the greatest,"
>   declares the LORD.

"For I will forgive their wickedness
     and will remember their sins no more."
     (Jeremiah 31:33-34)

This new covenant has already been inaugurated by Jesus Christ. Nonetheless, even after Jesus' death and resurrection and after the coming of the Holy Spirit, we still await its complete fulfillment. Life with God in his eternal city is yet to come.

The new covenant does, however, stand as a symbol of our status in history before God. We are always in receipt of many of God's promises—whether we are Jews in Egypt or Christians in the age before Christ's return. For us today, for example, the promised Messiah has come as the Savior and has rescued us from the consequences of sin. God is currently in the process of saving us from the power of sin, but he is yet to save us from the presence of sin. Some call this the *already but not yet* of human experience in God's world.

JESUS: THE RESCUE ASSURED

After the return of the Jews to Jerusalem, the biblical narrative is silent for about four hundred years. It is only (by our calendar) in about 7 BC, at a time when Israel was a part of the Roman Empire, that God again broke into history with the announcement of the birth of Jesus and of his forerunner, John the Baptist. Jesus was born of Mary, who was a virgin, and was conceived of the Holy Spirit. God thus began the final stage in saving his people. He became one of them, one of us. "The Word [God himself] became flesh and made his dwelling among us," says the Gospel of John. "We have seen his glory, the glory of the one and only Son, who came from the Father, full of grace and truth" (John 1:14).

Raised as a normal Jewish child, Jesus took to the road as an itinerant teacher when he was about thirty years old. He gathered around him a group of disciples, taught the people, healed the sick, and argued with the religious and political leaders of his day. Finally he became such a threat to both the political leaders (though Jesus was not interested in political power) and the religious authorities (though Jesus actually was the fulfillment of Old Testament prophecies concerning a Messiah who would save the people) that he had to be disposed of.

He was, therefore, tried for sedition. In what is the most outstanding miscarriage of justice in history, he was convicted and crucified. Three days later his grave was empty. He had been resurrected from the dead.

As the resurrected Lord, Jesus taught his followers for a few weeks and then ascended to the Father in heaven. As the disciples saw him disappear into the clouds, "Two men dressed in white stood beside them. 'Men of Galilee,' they said, 'why do you stand here looking into the sky? This same Jesus, who has been taken from you into heaven, will come back in the same way you have seen him go into heaven'" (Acts 1:10-11). Thus it is that Christians today still look forward to the Second Coming when Jesus will return at the end of history.

IN THE MIDDLE OF THINGS

The hand-in-hand but solitary way of the human race is, of course, not yet over. The church stands in the *already and not yet* flow of history. Already we are saved by God through the death of his Son; already we live under the reign of God as citizens of his kingdom. But not yet do we know God so well that none of us need teach our neighbor. Nor are we fully restored into the image of God as we were intended.

We still live in the middle of things. Looking back, we praise God, for searching us out and finding us. Looking forward in the company of all God's people, we have hope for eternal life.

QUESTIONS FOR REFLECTION

1. Why is Abraham important to the history of God's dealings with fallen humanity?

2. How do the following prefigure the sacrifice of Christ on the cross: the clothing of Adam and Eve after the fall, Abraham's near sacrifice of Isaac, and the sacrificial system of Leviticus 16?

3. To what extent does the pattern of the people of Israel in the wilderness appear in the twentieth century? Can you give any examples from your own experience?

4. Summarize the flow of biblical history from Saul to the fall of Jerusalem.

5. What was the basic message of the prophets?

6. How does the theme of the *already but not yet* show itself in Old Testament history, New Testament history, and contemporary life?

7. How was Jesus both the culmination of Jewish history and the foundation for the age of Christianity?

8. For one Old Testament summary of history, read Psalm 105. What is the purpose of this summary?

9. For one New Testament summary of biblical history read Stephen's sermon (Acts 6:8–8:1). What points is Stephen drawing from this survey? How are these received?

CHAPTER NINE

God's Finished Work

No more heinous crime was ever committed against God nor greater act of love consummated on behalf of the criminal. . . . "It is finished!" he cried. Completed. Done. Forever ended. He crashed through the gates of hell, set prisoners free, abolished death and burst in new life from the tomb. All to set you free from sin and open the way for you to run into the loving arms of God.

JOHN WHITE, *THE FIGHT*

THE CENTRAL EVENT IN human history took place about two thousand years ago. According to the Bible, all history looks either forward or backward to the death and resurrection of Jesus. What makes the cross the turning point in human events? Simple: it was there that God once and for all solved the human dilemma, the problem of sin and its consequence, death.

Let us take a closer look at this problem and then at the objective dimension of redemption—the finished work of Christ.

A DOUBLE DOSE OF DEATH

"The wages of sin is death" (Romans 6:23), wrote the apostle Paul. But what did he mean? What kind of death? We are all sinners, but we have not died. When Paul said that we are "dead in [our] transgressions and sins" (Ephesians 2:1), what did he have in mind? There must be more to death than physical death.

Indeed there is. The word *death* is used in two basic ways in the Bible. And though they are related, we need to distinguish carefully between them. The first sort of death is *physical death*, which we may think of as the separation of the "self" or the soul (who we are in ourselves) from the body. Physical death for human beings is not extinction of the personality. Rather, our "self" or soul continues to exist while the physical body decays.

The second kind of death is *spiritual death*. This too is a separation—a separation of the "self" or soul from God. This is the sort of death we experience even while physically alive. That is, our sin separates us from God and deprives us of our close personal relationship with him. God can brook no evil. Therefore, he severs his relationship with us and then lets us go on our own.

The irony is, however, that even then we are not on our own. Instead we follow "the ways of this world and of the ruler of the kingdom of the air, the spirit who is now at work in those who are disobedient" (Ephesians 2:2). We are "gratifying the cravings of our flesh and following its desires and thoughts." All of this makes us "deserving of wrath" (Ephesians 2:3)—that is, under the judgment of God. We are now dead (that is, personally separated from God) in our sins, and when we die physically we will be forever separated from God with no further chance to be made right before him. This is, of course, the meaning of hell. Hell is to be made in the image of God but to be forever separated from the reality of God—the only thing that makes the image meaningful. A mirror separated from any object to reflect is emptiness itself.

"People are destined to die once, and after that to face judgment," says the writer to the Hebrews (9:27). Or to paraphrase: we only live one physical life. When we die physically, we are judged on the basis of our spiritual condition at the time of our physical death. If we are still dead in our sins, our judgment will be to stay dead— separated from God forever. If we are alive spiritually, we will continue to live spiritually; that is, in close personal relationship to God.

GOD'S ANSWER TO OUR PROBLEM

The question is, therefore: How can we who are dead in our sins ever become alive? How can the wages of sin ever be paid in such a way that we no longer suffer their consequences? Let's consider the options:

1. The sinner himself receives these wages. If this happens, of course, the result is death—eternal separation from God. If we are to be made right with God, we cannot receive the just wages for our sin.

2. Some other person receives these wages for us. That might be possible if there were someone else who qualified. But everyone else is separated from God too. Other human beings must receive the wages for their own sin.

3. God himself receives the wages. Indeed! Precisely what is needed. We cannot solve our own dilemma. It must be solved for us.

Redemption is God in Christ receiving for us the wages of our sin. Here is how Paul explains redemption in one of the most thrilling sections of his letter to the Romans.

> You see, at just the right time, when we were still powerless, Christ died for the ungodly. Very rarely will anyone die for a righteous person, though for a good person someone

might possibly dare to die. But God demonstrates his own love for us in this: While we were still sinners, Christ died for us.

Since we have now been justified by his blood, how much more shall we be saved from God's wrath through him! (Romans 5:6-9)

Do you see what Paul has said? *While we were yet sinners, Christ died for us!* "God made him [Jesus] who had no sin to be sin for us, so that in him we might become the righteousness of God" (2 Corinthians 5:21). This is redemption—God in Christ doing for us what we could never in a million, million years do for ourselves.

GOD SO LOVED THE WORLD

And why did he do it? Because of his love. On the cross we see God's justice and God's mercy flow together. In his justice he sees our sins; he knows our corruption. He, more than we ever will, sees the venom of asps under our lips. This he knows demands judgment. But then in his love he himself takes on the punishment we deserve.

"'He [Christ] himself bore our sins' in his body on the cross," wrote the apostle Peter (1 Peter 2:24). And in his vision of the Suffering Servant the prophet Isaiah gave this vivid word picture:

But he was pierced for our transgressions,
    he was crushed for our iniquities;
the punishment that brought us peace was
        on him,
    and by his wounds we are healed.
We all, like sheep, have gone astray,
    each of us has turned to our own way;
and the LORD has laid on him
    the iniquity of us all. (Isaiah 53:5-6)

Many Bible scholars believe that the death Jesus died for our sins—the death that separated the Son from the Father, for that's what spiritual death involves—took place before his physical death. It is reflected when Jesus in the midst of his agony looked up from the cross and cried with a loud voice, "My God, my God, why have you forsaken me?" (Matthew 27:46). Jesus was expressing the fact of his separation from God—his spiritual death. After that came the words, "It is finished" (John 19:30), indicating that his main mission on earth was complete. He had paved the way for us to come back to God.

In the words of John Milton in *Paradise Lost*, God the Son had said to the Father,

Behold me then: me for him, life for life,
I offer, on me let thine anger fall;
Account me man. (III, 236-38)

And God did just this. But God the Father did not leave his Son forever separated from himself. Jesus' final words are, "Father, into your hands I commit my spirit" (Luke 23:46). Redemption had been accomplished. Jesus now died physically; his spirit (or soul) was separated from his body. Then Easter morning, three days later, Jesus rose from the dead as the "first fruit" of the resurrection, so guaranteeing our own later resurrection to life with God.

JUST AS IF I'D NEVER SINNED

Because Jesus died for us as our substitute, we are now in a very different position as human beings. Paul writes, "Since we have now been justified by his blood, how much more shall we be saved from God's wrath through him!" (Romans 5:9).

One little phrase in that sentence needs clarification: What does it mean to be *justified by his blood*? The blood refers to the kind of death Jesus died. But what does the word *justified* mean?

Justification is what God does for us in declaring us right before him. Because Jesus received the wages of our sin for us, for me, it is *just as if I'd never sinned*. That is, God has declared that we are *just* or *right* before him. He no longer sees us as sinners. The blood of Christ has cleansed us from all sins (1 John 1:7).

This, then, restores our personal relationship to God. God can now look on us not as sinners but as people for whom Christ died. He sees us, then, clothed in the robes of righteousness given to us by Jesus.

THE GREATEST STORY ONLY HALF TOLD

All of this happened some two thousand years ago. Haven't we gotten the message? Why do we not live as if God were truly our Father? What's missing? Why do so many of us feel dead to God?

The answer is simple. Not only does redemption have an objective dimension, it has a subjective dimension as well. God does not just redeem mankind in general; he brings new spiritual life to individuals. For each of us to reflect the image of God we need individually to bow before Jesus Christ and accept him as our Savior and Lord. But this is to anticipate the next chapter.

QUESTIONS FOR REFLECTION

1. If redemption is the answer to a problem, what is the problem?

2. Define the two kinds of death. What do they hold in common? How are they different?

3. How did God solve the problem of human sin and death (Romans 5:6-11)?

4. Could *any* person solve it? Why or why not?

5. How are God's justice and mercy brought together in the death and resurrection of Jesus? How is justice satisfied? How is his love expressed?

6. What does it mean to be justified by Jesus' blood?

7. Read Isaiah 53. Picture the scene envisioned there. Give thanks to God for his great love.

8. Have you experienced justification or are you still dead through your trespasses and sins? Are you under the penalty of death? For your personal way out, read the next chapter.

CHAPTER TEN

New Life in Christ

Thou hast made me, and shall Thy worke decay?
Repaire me now, for now mine end doth haste,
I runne to death, and death meets me as fast,
And all my pleasures are like yesterday;
I dare not move my dimme eyes any way,
Despaire behind, and death before doth cast
Such terrour, and my feeble flesh doth waste
By sinne in it, which it t'wards hell doth weigh;
Onley Thou art above, and when towards thee
By Thy leave I can looke, I rise again;
But our old subtle foe so tempteth me
That not one houre my selfe I can sustain;
Thy Grace may wing me to prevent his art,
And Thou like Adamant draw mine iron heart.

JOHN DONNE, "HOLY SONNET I"

THE SUMMER BEFORE I was to enter the seventh grade our family moved from a ranch in northern Nebraska to the county seat of a neighboring county. In the country I had ridden a pony over two miles to a proverbial one-room schoolhouse. Since we lived twenty miles from the nearest town, we never went to church. My parents were

Christians, however, and I and my sisters received some Sunday school instruction from my mother.

Occasionally during the summer months a minister from one of the churches in a nearby town would hold services on Sunday afternoon in a country schoolhouse, and then our family would attend. But I didn't learn much as a young child about God and his ways with his wayward creation.

When we moved to town, however, things changed. We lived just across the street from the Butte Community Church. Every Sunday a young pastor, Ward Smith, explained the good news to the good people of my farming and ranching community.

It was then that I learned about God and what my sins did to my relationship to him. It didn't take much to convince me I was in bad shape. In fact, within a couple of months, I felt so burdened by my separation from God that on one hot Sunday morning, during the altar call, I fainted.

The congregation was singing a hymn, perhaps "Just As I Am," and I knew that I should move out of the pew, walk down the aisle and tell the pastor I needed help in getting right with God. Instead, I just passed out.

My father and a couple of other men picked me up and carried me across the street to our home. I was conscious by the time they had deposited me on a couch.

During this time the people around me were saying, "Oh! It's so hot today. He was just overcome by the heat." And, "It was just too stuffy in church today. He'll soon be okay."

But I vividly remember my mother putting all these comments aside, leaning over the couch after everyone else had left and asking, "Was it something the preacher said?"

"Yes, Mama," I answered. "I thought so," she said and left it at that.

The next Sunday, when I was again given the chance to respond, I quickly left my pew and met with Pastor Smith. It is to this time and place I will always point as the turning point in my life with God. It marks for me the beginning of new spiritual life.

Many Christians can mark their new birth in space and time as I can. They know just when and where their relationship to God was changed. Many Christians cannot mark so clearly either time or place. Looking back on their past life, they see, perhaps, a period of time in which new life seemed to come to them. Others only know that whatever the past was like, they know now that they are living under the lordship of Christ, that he is indeed their Savior.

So I do not tell this story to serve as a model. It is only an example of what happened to one person God brought back into close personal relationship with himself. The reason I tell this story is to testify to God's life-changing role in my life, and to encourage each of you as readers to pursue your own way toward God so that God might find you too.

The Bible has many accounts of people who have encountered God in life-transforming ways. We saw how God changed Moses' life in chapter two. Here we will see how Jesus challenged Nicodemus, a ruler among the Jews, to a brand new life from above.

YOU MUST BE BORN AGAIN

When Pastor Smith spoke with me after the church service that Sunday morning in July, he showed me several verses in the Bible. One of them is set in the context of the story of Nicodemus who comes to Jesus because he believes him to be a teacher sent from God. (It would be helpful here if you would read the entire story in your Bible, John 3:1-21.)

Jesus wasted no time getting directly to Nicodemus's problem. Nicodemus didn't know it, but he needed to be "born anew" or, as it can also be translated, "born again" (John 3:3). When

Jesus told him this, however, Nicodemus didn't even know what Jesus was talking about.

"What do you mean?" he asked. "Must I go back to my mother's womb?"

But Jesus went on to explain that every person needs two births: a physical birth (Nicodemus was okay here) and a spiritual birth (Nicodemus was as yet unborn in this sense).

Nicodemus was still baffled by Jesus' explanation, so Jesus gave an illustration. He likened the movement of the Spirit that gives spiritual birth to the movement of the wind. Picture a field of golden wheat ripe for harvest under a summer sun. It's not still, but moving and shifting in waves that ripple from one end of the field to the other. We don't see the wind, but we see its effect.

So it is with spiritual life. We do not see a spiritual pipeline stretching up from the earth past the galaxies to God. But we see the effect of God's action in our lives. We come to know God personally. His Holy Spirit dwells in the heart of each believer. As the apostle Paul writes, God's Spirit bears witness with our spirit and we then cry, "Abba! Father!" (Romans 8:15-16). That is, we know God so intimately we rightfully call him, "Papa! Daddy!"

Being born spiritually, then, puts us in a new family. We now have both a physical father and a spiritual father. As normal children we were born into the human family. As young Christians we are born into the family of God. This has tremendous ramifications. It means not only a new father but also a new and huge set of brothers and sisters in Christ. That is what the church in general is—our new family, the people of God.

THE WAY TO SPIRITUAL LIFE

Jesus' challenge to Nicodemus is, therefore, to be born anew, born from above. But, Nicodemus might well ask, how do I go about this?

Jesus has an answer. Because he was speaking to an educated Jew, he referred Nicodemus to the Old Testament. "You remember the story of Moses and the serpent," Jesus said. Nicodemus would be able to recall the account in Numbers 21:4-9. The Israelites were in the desert and complained because of lack of water and good food. So God sent poisonous serpents that bit many of the people so that they died. Then the people realized they had spoken too soon against God. They therefore repented, saying to Moses, "We sinned when we spoke against the LORD and against you. Pray that the LORD will take the snakes away from us" (Numbers 21:7).

Then God provided a way out. Moses was to make a bronze serpent and place it on a stick.

Whoever would look at the serpent would be healed of his snakebite.

This account in Numbers stands as an allegory or parable of new birth. Like the Israelites we have been bitten by the serpent of sin and will surely die if we do not receive a cure. Again like the Israelites we cannot cure ourselves. Only God can cure us. The story is symbolic in another way, as well. Our salvation rests on the crucifixion of Christ on the cross. It is only as we look in faith to him that we can be given new life.

Notice that the Israelites needed to respond in two ways. First, they needed to repent of their sins; that is, they needed to see themselves as sinners before a holy God, to be deeply sorry for their own unholy state, and be ready to live lives obedient to God. To repent means to turn around, to reverse direction.

Second, they needed to trust the remedy provided by God. The act of looking is not the act of doing good works or piling up good deeds or going through a ritual or attending a church or meditating in silence for years on end. It is simply an act of faith.

John the Gospel writer goes on to explain the import of both Nicodemus's story and the story of the serpent. He does so in the words my pastor used to help me know how I could be born again: "For God so loved the world that he gave his one and only Son, that whoever believes in him shall not perish but have eternal life" (John 3:16). This has sometimes been called the gospel (good news) in a nutshell—an apt description. It tells us of God's love for us, his recognition that we need a desperate remedy for our desperate plight, his provision of that remedy, and our response.

That response is captured in the phrase *believe in him*. That is, whoever recognizes his own bleak situation before God and trusts in Jesus Christ to bring him to new life will indeed receive that life. And when spiritual life begins, it never ends. It's eternal.

Because Jesus gives new life to those who *believe in him*, some people mistakenly assume that not much commitment is expected on the part of the believer. We should be aware of how Jesus treated such would-be followers.

A rich man once approached Jesus, knelt before him, and asked, "Good teacher, what must I do to inherit eternal life?" (Mark 10:17). When Jesus discerned that this man's central sin was his love for money, "Jesus looked at him and loved him. 'One thing you lack,' he said. 'Go, sell everything you have and give to the poor, and you will have treasure in heaven. Then come, follow me'" (Mark 10:21). The man went away in sorrow. For him, wealth was more important than following Jesus.

It is not only love of money that can stand in the way of true repentance. Luke writes,

> As they were walking along the road, a man said to him, "I will follow you wherever you go."
>
> Jesus replied, "Foxes have dens and birds have nests, but the Son of Man has no place to lay his head."
>
> He said to another man, "Follow me."
>
> But he replied, "Lord, first let me go and bury my father."
>
> Jesus said to him, "Let the dead bury their own dead, but you go and proclaim the kingdom of God."
>
> Still another said, "I will follow you, Lord; but first let me go back and say goodbye to my family."
>
> Jesus replied, "No one who puts a hand to the plow and looks back is fit for service in the kingdom of God." (Luke 9:57-62)

In a simple, straightforward way, Jesus challenged three people with the cost of discipleship. To one the issue was comfort; to the other two the ties to friends and family.

In a parable Jesus likened following him to building a tower. Before beginning, one needs to count the cost, lest only the foundation be laid before the money runs out (Luke 14:28-29). Likewise, Jesus said, a king whose kingdom is attacked needs to see if he has sufficient troops to wage successfully even a defensive war (Luke 14:31-32). A person should count the cost before setting forth on the Christian way. And what is the cost?

Jesus' words are striking: "Those of you who do not give up everything you have cannot be my disciples" (Luke 14:33). Jesus cannot be our Savior without being our Lord. We cannot be born again without living out that new spiritual life.

We do not know much about Nicodemus's immediate response to Jesus. But we do know that later as Jesus was arguing vigorously with the religious leaders, Nicodemus stood on Jesus' side (John 7:50). And we know that after the crucifixion Nicodemus came with a mixture of myrrh and aloes to anoint Jesus' body for burial (John 19:39). Hardly the acts of one who wanted to avoid the cost of discipleship!

That morning in Nebraska, many years ago, I believed in Jesus. I didn't know all that it meant. I didn't know all that it would cost. But I repented of my sins, trusted in Christ, and began to follow his way. God has brought me to new life. He has made me his child, adopted me into his family. He is my Father. Praise God!

YOUR MOVE

If you have not experienced this, if you cannot call God your Father by the witness of the Holy Spirit, you should know that nothing stands in the way of that but you. You can be born again now. It's your move.

If you are not sure you are God's child, if there is any doubt, you can remove that uncertainty now.

I would urge anyone who wishes to come to God—for the first time or, for the record, a second time—to read and study the following prayer. If you believe it expresses your deepest desire, make this prayer your own and pray it quietly and aloud to God.

Heavenly Father, I know that without you I am dead in sin. I am not naturally alive. I am not naturally your child. I know that I put myself first and do not love you as I should or obey your commandments as I should. I know that because of this I do not deserve your love or forgiveness. I deserve to be separated from you forever.

I also know that Jesus Christ, your Son, has died for me. He has paid my penalty of death. I believe in him and place my trust in him.

And so I give myself to you as much as I know how and accept Jesus not only as my Savior but as my Lord. I want to follow you all the days of my life and so to find life in you throughout eternity.

Please accept me as one of your children and live in me by your Holy Spirit.

In the name of Jesus Christ, Amen.

There is no magic in this or any other prayer. Praying it without meaning it, praying it without following through and acting like a child of God, will not merit anything. You may even be in worse condition because you may think this prayer has somehow earned you a place with God.

Nothing earns you life with God. Only God can give this life and he gives it only to those who are serious about their faith. No one can fool around with God.

But—and what a tremendous *but* it is—John the Gospel writer has great words of encouragement to those who have received Jesus as their Savior and Lord: "To all who did receive him, to those who believed in his name, he gave the right to become children of God." For those new children of God are born "not of . . . human decision or a husband's will, but born of God" (John 1:12-13).

This was the second section of Scripture I remember Pastor Smith sharing with me. It gave me confidence then. I trust it will give you confidence now.

Jesus is our Lord and Savior. We are his children, not because we willed it, but because he did! God is our Father because he wants to be. Praise God!

QUESTIONS FOR REFLECTION

It is essential to understand redemption as the answer to humanity's most basic problem. So answer the first four questions as a summary of what we have studied in the past few chapters.

1. What is humankind's (yours, mine, everyone's) basic problem?

2. What can any person (or all of us put together) do about it?

3. What has God done about it?

4. Is this all there is to it? Is God's plan for salvation automatic?

5. Read John 3:1-21. Who is Nicodemus (vv. 1, 10)?

6. When he comes to Jesus, what does he already believe about him (v. 2)?

7. How does Jesus respond? What does this indicate about what Jesus knew about Nicodemus's real need?

8. Does Nicodemus understand Jesus' response (v. 4)? Was Nicodemus not very bright? How would you respond if someone told you, "You must be born again"?

9. What kind of birth is the old (first) birth?

10. What kind of birth is the new (second) birth?

11. How many times had Nicodemus been born?

12. How many times have you been born?

13. How does Jesus describe the activity of the Spirit (v. 8)? Who is in control of the wind's activity? Who is in control of the Spirit's activity?

14. What is Jesus saying about himself in verse 13? Who is he claiming to be? What authority is he claiming to have?

15. Read Numbers 21:4-9. In light of this passage, what does Jesus mean in John 3:14? How was the "Son of man" (Jesus) lifted up?

16. Read John 3:16-21 carefully again. What motivated God to send his Son?

17. What is required of each person?

18. What is the result of "believing in him"?

19. What does it mean to "believe in him"? What if a person does not believe in him?

20. What does repentance mean?

How do the following passages emphasize the cost of discipleship: Mark 10:17-31, Luke 9:57-62, and Luke 14:25-33? What do they say about the benefits of discipleship?

21. What is your own response to Jesus' offer of eternal life? Are you believing in him now? Are you ready to begin to believe in him? What does repentance mean in your life?

22. What confidence does John 1:12 give those who believe in Jesus?

CHAPTER ELEVEN

A New Lifestyle

And we all, who with unveiled faces contemplate the Lord's glory, are being transformed into his image with ever-increasing glory, which comes from the Lord, who is the Spirit.

2 CORINTHIANS 3:18

WHEN I PLACED MY FAITH in Jesus Christ so many years ago in Nebraska, I had no idea what was in store for me. I know now that my life would have been very different if I had remained as I was then—apart from God.

The good news about what God has done for us in Jesus Christ does not end with the fact of the new birth. The new birth is just the beginning.

LOTS OF GOOD NEWS

You will recall that the first good news we learned about ourselves is that as human beings we are made in the image of God. This gives us value, dignity, worth. Then we learned the bad news that in the fall that image was impaired, defaced, like a coin that has been run over by a locomotive.

We can still see vestiges of the image, but it's all been twisted out of shape.

Now we have the second major piece of good news: through the new birth the image of God is being restored in us. The apostle Paul, writing to the Corinthians, says, "We all, who with unveiled faces contemplate the Lord's glory, are being transformed into his image with ever-increasing glory, which comes from the Lord, who is the Spirit" (2 Corinthians 3:18). Or in his letter to the Romans, he writes that we are "predestined to be conformed to the image of his Son" (Romans 8:29; see also 1 Corinthians 15:49). God has had it in mind all along to restore us to our likeness to him.

We have, therefore, been given a new life—a spiritual life, a life of close personal relationship with God our Father. "If anyone is in Christ," Paul says, "the new creation has come: The old has gone, the new is here!" (2 Corinthians 5:17). Through the work of his Holy Spirit in our lives we are being changed into people worthy of the name *children of God*.

The process by which God begins to restore in us the image of his Son is called, in theological terms, *sanctification*. Sanctification saves us from the power of sin in our lives, just as salvation (or rebirth) saves us from the consequences of sin.

NEW LIFE, NEW LIFESTYLE

In picturing the progress of the Christian life, the New Testament takes two parallel tracks. On the one hand, the new life begun at the new birth is a gift from God. It is seen as God living in believers, changing them, molding them, transforming them into new persons—the ones they were designed to be from the beginning, fully reflecting God in all they do.

"I have been crucified with Christ," says Paul, "and I no longer live, but Christ lives in me" (Galatians 2:20). Or again, "For to me, to live is Christ" (Philippians 1:21).

On the other hand, the New Testament encourages, challenges, entreats, and commands us to live a life worthy of that to which we are called. The process of sanctification, in other words, is not totally out of our hands. As we have been given dominion as a part of the image of God, so God expects us to exercise that dominion in our own lives.

The letter to the Galatians is written with just this situation in mind. As Christians we are free from the bondage of the law. The fact that as sinners we have broken that law is no longer held against us. But this does not give us license to live any way we choose. We are called to freedom, but we are not to use that freedom to follow along in the pattern of our former sinful lifestyle.

Think about it. Does it make sense for those with new life to continue to live as if nothing had happened? From new life comes a whole new lifestyle.

THE FIGHT

It is, nonetheless, true that the process is not automatic. We are not transformed in the twinkling of an eye. For we are still surrounded by sin in our environment. And, what is more troublesome, we are still plagued by our old habits and our old, rebellious, self-serving nature. Paul calls this our "flesh."

In Galatians Paul challenges us. Let us look in some detail at what he says:

> So I say, walk by the Spirit, and you will not gratify the desires of the flesh. For the flesh desires what is contrary to the Spirit, and the Spirit what is contrary to the flesh. They are in conflict with each other, so that you are not to do whatever you want. But if you are led by the Spirit, you are not under the law.
>
> The acts of the flesh are obvious: sexual immorality, impurity and debauchery; idolatry and witchcraft; hatred, discord,

jealousy, fits of rage, selfish ambition, dissensions, factions and envy; drunkenness, orgies, and the like. I warn you, as I did before, that those who live like this will not inherit the kingdom of God.

But the fruit of the Spirit is love, joy, peace, forbearance, kindness, goodness, faithfulness, gentleness and self-control. Against such things there is no law. Those who belong to Christ Jesus have crucified the flesh with its passions and desires. Since we live by the Spirit, let us keep in step with the Spirit. (Galatians 5:16-25)

Paul makes it clear that we have a fight on our hands. The Spirit, the Holy Spirit who dwells in us as Christians and is changing us into his likeness, is at war with the flesh. Remember that by *flesh* Paul does not mean simply the body. He means our rebellious nature—anything in us that urges us to go against God, anything that draws us toward selfishness and triviality. A battle is going on in us—our good side against our bad. And Paul challenges us to be led by the Spirit and to follow, in the midst of trial and trouble, the path of truth and righteousness.

THE WORKS OF THE FLESH

Notice how specific Paul becomes. There is no reason for us to wonder what the wrong course for our life is. The works of the flesh are clearly identified: *sexual immorality, impurity, debauchery, idolatry, witchcraft, hatred, discord, jealousy, rage, selfish ambition, dissensions, factions, envy, drunkenness,* and *orgies.*

What a list of "fleshly" characteristics! And yet Paul admits that even this long list is not complete, for he adds "and the like." Let me ask you to reflect for a few moments on each of the items. Consult a dictionary if some of the terms are vague to you. Which of them characterize your life? Which give you at least some difficulty? Are you free from any? (If so, praise God, but be careful not to stumble.)

Paul's comment on this list is awesome: "I warn you, as I warned you before, that those who do such things shall not inherit the kingdom of God" (Galatians 5:21 NIV 1984). Does this mean no sinner ever enters heaven? No. *Only* sinners enter heaven—saved sinners. Paul is pointing out to us that if our lives are characterized by such continued sins, we may not be born again after all. As John Stott points out, the phrase "do such things" should better be rendered "habitually do such things." To have our lives marked by these works of our lower nature is to give evidence that we are not right with God in the first place. If we find ourselves in this situation, we should go back to square one—where we may never have gone before—and place our lives in God's care, repenting of our sins and believing in Christ, as we explained in the previous chapter.

THE FRUIT OF THE SPIRIT

The sanctified life, that is, the life given over to the expression of the new life, the life in the Spirit, is also clearly pictured by Paul. He says our lives should be marked by the fruit of the Spirit: *love, joy, peace, forbearance (patience), kindness, goodness, faithfulness, gentleness,* and *self-control.*

What a contrast to the works of the flesh! Indeed, for they flow from the work of the Holy Spirit in our lives.

Contemplate this list, too. Which ones are most fully expressed in your life? Where do you need help? Every time you evidence any of these you are bearing the fruit of the Spirit: this is what God wants you to be like. This is what he is transforming you to be. You are being "transformed into his image with ever-increasing glory" (2 Corinthians 3:18). One day your whole life will be filled with the fruit of the Spirit.

There is something striking about both these lists. Nowhere in any of them do we find a hint of what sort of job or task we as Christians are going to be called to do. To become a Christian does not mean one stops being an accountant, a student, a clerk, a spouse, a grocer, or a computer nerd.

God is not primarily interested in our occupation. He is interested in our character: who we are, not in how we come to express this in action. We are to be loving in everything, patient in everything, peaceful in everything, and so on. To be these things is to be like Jesus Christ. Think about each of these fruits. Do they not describe our Lord? His life is one specific expression of all these fruits of the Spirit. To imitate him is to bear such fruit.

The Bible has much, much more to say about our sanctification than I am able to mention or discuss here. I would, therefore, direct your attention especially to the following sections of Paul's letters. Colossians 3:1–4:6 is a passage parallel to the one we have just discussed, but it goes deeper and takes up specific issues of our attitude to the family and to servitude. Romans 12:1–15:13 also outlines the new lifestyle and examines our relationship to the state. Titus 2–3 is also helpful. The whole of 1 John explains how our lives are to be filled with love. And the entire book of James tells us how to put our faith into action.

THE MEANS OF GRACE

After Jesus ascended to the Father, the disciples remained for a while in Jerusalem. Then, as Jesus predicted (Acts 1:8), the Holy Spirit came upon the believers and they became his witnesses first in Jerusalem and then throughout the surrounding area and eventually into all the world. The Holy Spirit still lives in his believers today, empowering them to live lives worthy of God and to spread the good news about Jesus.

The Holy Spirit uses several means of effecting transformation of the believer. The first is corporate worship. The followers of Jesus constantly came together to praise God in psalms and spiritual songs, to pray as a body, to hear the teaching of the apostles, to baptize, to celebrate the Lord's Supper, and, in general, to express corporately to God their growing sense of his glory. The writer to the Hebrews makes this traditional practice a command: "Let us hold unswervingly to the hope we profess," he writes, "for he who promised is faithful. And let us consider how we may spur one another on toward love and good deeds, not giving up meeting together, as some are in the habit of doing, but encouraging one another—and all the more as you see the Day [of Christ's coming] approaching" (Hebrews 10:23-25).

As the Bible became available to a wider group of people, it also became possible for Christians to read and study it individually as well as corporately. For centuries Christians have set aside a time each day for private reading of the Bible and for private prayer. Daily devotions or a daily quiet time provide an important way for Christians to follow Jesus' instructions to new believers: "If you hold to my teaching, you are really my disciples. Then you will know the truth, and the truth will set you free" (John 8:31-32). Through daily reading of God's Word and daily putting it into action, God will indeed set us free from sin and restore his image in us.

When we talk with God, we should make our prayers full-orbed. They should be marked by *adoration* of God, expressing to God what we know of who he is and praising him for this. *Confession* of our failures should be made. *Thanksgiving* for what God has done and is doing should begin to flow naturally from us. Finally we may round out our prayers with *supplication,* in which we make our requests for others and for ourselves known to God.

ALL IS OF GRACE

As we have concentrated in this chapter on new life in Christ—on what should typify the character of the Christian—we should never forget our debt to Christ. Our life, our good deeds done in the Spirit as Christians, our worship, Bible study, and prayer, do not justify us before God.

Some things, in other words, bear repeating. God is the initiator, the active one not only in our creation but also in our re-creation and in our continued new life. The clearest expression of this is in Ephesians 2:8-10:

> For it is by grace you have been saved, through faith—and this is not from yourselves, it is the gift of God—not by works, so that no one can boast. For we are God's handiwork, created in Christ Jesus to do good works, which God prepared in advance for us to do.

This marvelous passage puts together two sides of our Christian experience. First, we are saved by *grace* which, simply put, means "God's unmerited favor toward us." While we were yet sinners—and didn't deserve salvation—Christ died for us. We received our salvation as a gift. We held out our empty hands in faith; God placed there the gift of his salvation.

Second, we are created to *do good works.* In fact, God has prepared these for us long before we ever get around to doing them. We are to work out our salvation "with fear and trembling, for it is God who works in you to will and to act in order to fulfill his good purpose" (Philippians 2:12-13). The sovereignty of God has, therefore, encompassed our justification before him, our new birth, and our new life. So even our good works are of grace. Or, as the Puritans so frequently used to say, all is of grace—our new life, our new lifestyle.

QUESTIONS FOR REFLECTION

1. What is the New Testament basis for the idea that with new life comes the restoration of the image of God in a person?

2. Recall the characteristics of the image of God as outlined in chapter five. How may new Christians expect their lives to change?

3. What role does God play in the new life of a Christian? What role does the Christian play?

4. How does Paul characterize the old lifestyle in Galatians 5:19-21? Do any of these mark your life? What should you do about it?

5. What characterizes the new lifestyle (Galatians 5:22-23)?

6. What means to the new lifestyle has God provided?

7. What further light on the new life is shed by the Scripture passages mentioned on the pages that follow?

8. Read Ephesians 2:1-10. What does the word *grace* mean as it is used in verses 5, 7, and 8?

9. Examine verses Ephesians 2:8-10 carefully. How does salvation come? What role is played by each of the following: (1) grace, (2) faith, and (3) good works?

CHAPTER TWELVE

Jesus the Christ

Come to me, all you who are weary and burdened, and I will give you rest. Take my yoke upon you and learn from me, for I am gentle and humble in heart, and you will find rest for your souls. For my yoke is easy and my burden is light.

MATTHEW 11:28-30

SO FAR IN THIS BOOK we have considered the Christian faith as a system of beliefs—beliefs about God, about ourselves, about the world around us, and how all of these interrelate. Especially, we have been concerned with beliefs about how we relate to God. But the Christian faith, while it involves a system of beliefs, is primarily about a personal relationship with Jesus Christ, the Son of God himself. For each of us to grow as Christians day by day, we must get to know and love him as a Person.

Indeed, God is personal and we can know and relate to him person to Person. This is one of the amazing truths of the Christian faith. God wants us to know him just as I want my daughters Carol and Ann and my sons Gene and Richard to know me. We saw how God spoke personally to Moses in the wilderness, through the voice out of the burning bush and the voice on the mountain. We have heard God's words through Moses and the prophets. But with the birth of Jesus we get to know God in fully human form.

Here is how the writer to the Hebrews put it:

> In the past God spoke to our ancestors through the prophets at many times and in various ways, but in these last days he has spoken to us by his Son, whom he appointed heir of all things, and through whom also he made the universe. (Hebrews 1:1-2)

In Jesus God has spoken in a profoundly clear and human way. As Jesus told his disciple Philip, "Anyone who has seen me has seen the Father" (John 14:9). And the risen Christ speaks in a vision to the apostle John, "Here I am! I stand at the door and knock. If anyone hears my voice and opens the door, I will come in and eat with that person, and they with me" (Revelation 3:20). Fellowship around a dining table is an image of deep personal acceptance and love.

So God has already made himself known to us. We only need to receive him, fellowship with him, and learn his character and his ways. The most obvious way to do this is to read the Gospels. They tell the story of Jesus' life and record for us his teachings. When we do this with an inquisitive mind and a loving heart, we will be amazed at what we find.

THE AMAZING JESUS

There are a huge number of books about Jesus. Every year sees a host of new attempts to capture the essence of his character or disclose the depths of his teaching. But none of these can ever replace the four Gospels of Matthew, Mark, Luke, and John. These books are indeed not just the prime source of our knowledge of Jesus; they are almost the only source. And what a rich resource they are! Scholars have been plumbing their depths for centuries, demonstrating their reliability as historical records and elaborating and explaining their meaning. But the delightful thing about them is that they are accessible to the simplest mind and inexhaustible by the profoundest intellect. What is more important, they reveal Jesus. The Spirit of God speaks through these Gospels directly to our hearts and minds and brings Jesus to us. Through the Holy Spirit we then can address God as Abba, Father, and Jesus as Lord, Savior, and even as friend.

Whom then do we meet in the Gospels? If we follow the progress of the disciples' understanding as it is displayed in the Gospel of Mark, for example, we first meet an enigma. To his disciples Jesus was both an ordinary man and a puzzling mystery. In the opening verses Mark announces his topic—the "gospel" (good news) of Jesus Christ, the Son of God. So from the beginning we see that this will be no simple tale of a human hero. It will be the tale of God's very Son. Mark then quickly proclaims his story as a fulfillment of prophecy, introduces John the Baptist as a forerunner of Jesus, tells of Jesus' baptism and temptation in the wilderness by Satan, and brings Jesus on stage as a preacher in Galilee. His message is bold: "The time has come. . . . The kingdom of God has come near. Repent and believe the good news!" (Mark 1:15).

In the next few lines of text Jesus calls the first four disciples, exorcizes several demonic spirits, heals his disciple Peter's mother-in-law, goes on a preaching tour in Galilee, and heals a leper. It is a common experience for those reading the Gospel of Mark for the first time to pause after the first couple of brief chapters and say, "Wow! Who is this guy? I thought Jesus was a meek, simple-minded lover of children and little animals, spouting nice Hallmark greeting card words of peace and comfort. Here he is, an ordinary man from the backwater town of Nazareth, commanding spirits, telling rough fisherman to follow him and become fishers of men, astounding the synagogue worshipers with his authority, and generally causing a stir up and down the whole territory from Jerusalem to Capernaum. People from all over Israel were flocking to hear him."

THE MOST ASTOUNDING THING ABOUT JESUS

Undoubtedly, the most astounding thing about Jesus was the natural, almost casual, way he displayed his divine character. He did not often declare in so many words that he was the Son of God or equal to God. He let his actions and his engagement and dialogues with people display who he was. He did this in such a way that, if we pay attention and are open to seeing, we cannot miss the implication that Jesus thought of himself—and displayed himself to be—someone with a very special relation to God. Take one of the early events in Jesus life as Mark recounts it in Mark 2:1-12.

Jesus had been traveling in Israel and had returned to his home in Capernaum, a town on the north shore of the Lake of Galilee. So many people had gathered there that the room in which he was teaching was packed. Four men then came carrying a paralyzed man on a cot. When they couldn't get in, they went to the roof of the house—roofs of houses in Galilee were flat—opened it up and let the man down in front of Jesus. Jesus, recognizing the faith of the four, looked at the paralyzed man and said, "Son, your sins are forgiven."

Now, think about it. Was this the reason he was brought to Jesus—to have his sins forgiven? Surely, the four men and the paralyzed man must have been surprised and disappointed. One can imagine them wanting to say, "Jesus, that's not what we want. We want him healed. We've heard that you have the power. Won't you do that for our friend?" But before they could respond, the religious leaders who were there began to ponder how Jesus could claim to forgive sins. Isn't that the prerogative of God alone? They were right, of course; only the one sinned against can forgive that sin. The man had not sinned against Jesus; he had sinned against God.

Jesus knew what these religious leaders were thinking. So he asked them, "Which is easier: to say to this paralyzed man, 'Your sins are forgiven,' or to say, 'Get up, take your mat and walk'?" Well, we think as readers, both of them sound quite impossible! But Jesus quickly added, "But I want you theologians and everyone else to know that I have authority on earth to forgive sins. So, you there on the cot, 'get up, take your mat and go home.'" And the man did just that.

The response of the crowd was utter amazement. "We have never seen anything like this!" they said.

But the amazement was due not primarily to Jesus' power to heal. There had been other healers in Israel. It was Jesus' implicit claim to have the power and the authority to forgive sins. By the time the disciples were made fully aware of who Jesus was—the very Son of God, the one whose death on the cross paid for the sins of the paralyzed man and all mankind—they would see that it was completely reasonable and appropriate for Jesus to say, "Your sins are forgiven." But at the time what a mystery it must have been! There was no question in the disciples' minds that Jesus was an ordinary man who walked as they walked, got tired and thirsty as they did, attended synagogue as they did, prayed as they prayed.

At the same time, there was no question that Jesus was someone very special, with a consciousness of the presence of God that they longed for but did not possess. Indeed, on the one hand, he was an ordinary teacher, teaching many of the truths they knew or were reminded of from Scripture. In some ways he taught like the rabbis, asking questions, preaching (as in the Sermon on the Mount in Matthew 5–7), and telling stories. On the other hand, he often taught in ways that were unique. Many of his stories were not quite like the stories of the rabbis.

JESUS' PARABLES

When people asked him questions, he often replied with questions that led to his telling a story that not only taught a lesson but also put the listeners in a position where they had to decide and often to act. Take the case of the expert in Jewish law who wanted to test Jesus' ability to answer tough questions. You will find this story in Luke 10:25-28.

The lawyer began by posing a highly significant question. "Teacher," he asked, "What must I do to inherit eternal life?"

Jesus replied with a question: "What is written in the Law?"

The man answered by quoting Scripture: "'Love the Lord your God with all your heart and with all your soul and with all your strength and with all your mind'; and, 'Love your neighbor as yourself.'" And Jesus immediately agreed, commending him for his answer.

Then Jesus added, "Do this and you will live."

This seems at first like an obvious response. But the lawyer had a problem with it. Jesus was asking the man to live up to the extent of his own knowledge, and he knew he wasn't doing this. After all, no one could live so perfectly. So he asked Jesus a further question: "Who is my neighbor?" He was looking for a reasonable limitation to the extent of his love. After all, he couldn't love everybody equally, could he? Surely, he would not need to love someone outside his own family or his own community as much as he loved those close to him.

But Jesus saw into his heart and told a story that put the lawyer in a position either to admit his own moral failure or to live consistently with his own sense of right and wrong. He told the story of the Good Samaritan, now a classic example of how Jesus often taught:

A man was going down from Jerusalem to Jericho, when he was attacked by robbers. They stripped him of his clothes, beat him and went away, leaving him half dead. A priest happened to be going down the same road, and when he saw the man, he passed by on the other side. So too, a Levite, when he came to the place and saw him, passed by on the other side. But a Samaritan, as he traveled, came where the man was;

and when he saw him, he took pity on him. He went to him and bandaged his wounds, pouring on oil and wine. Then he put the man on his own donkey, brought him to an inn and took care of him. The next day he took out two denarii[e] and gave them to the innkeeper. 'Look after him,' he said, 'and when I return, I will reimburse you for any extra expense you may have.' (Luke 10:30-35)

Then Jesus asked the man a simple question: "Which of these three do you think was a neighbor to the man who fell into the hands of robbers?"

The answer was obvious—but maddening. Jesus had made the Samaritan—a person in a despised ethnic group—the hero of the story. The lawyer is so disturbed by this that he doesn't call him "the Samaritan." He just says, "The one who had mercy on him." But that does not get him off the hook.

For Jesus says, "Go and do likewise." The lawyer had set out to put Jesus on the spot, possibly to show the crowd that he was the expert and Jesus was not. But Jesus left him hanging by his own rope. He either had to reform his life or cease claiming expertise as a student of the law, risking as well his own salvation.

What an amazingly attractive person Jesus is, we think after seeing how brilliantly he turned the tables on the expert! How ingenious for Jesus to make a Samaritan the hero! Today it would be like a Jewish teacher in Israel making a Palestinian the hero in a similar story. How clever not to engage in argument but to tell a story that made his points so dramatically surprising—and clear! Who could miss the message?

Well, we could miss the message, and many of us do. For the typical way people read the parable of the Good Samaritan is to say that Jesus is teaching that everyone is our neighbor. But, if we should think so, let us look again. Jesus does not extend the category of *neighbor* to include Samaritans. In the parable the neighbor is not the man who needs help. It is the Samaritan himself. The Jew is to be like the Samaritan! "Who is my neighbor?" is the wrong question. The point for *us* is to be a neighbor.

Who is your despised category of people? Is it some ethnic group, a high-school clique, an intellectual class, a social or political class? How would Jesus tell the story to you?

The parable is at once a rejection of ethnic superiority, a lesson in compassion, and, for the lawyer and us who read the story, a challenge to be neighbors. The message that we are not to be just hearers of the word but doers as well comes in power.

JESUS' PARABLES AND US

Jesus told many stories similar to this one. If we have been raised in the church, we may think we know them and what they mean. Let me challenge you to look again.

In the classic parable of the prodigal son (Luke 15:11-32), who are you most like—the younger wayward brother or the older faithful brother? Most of us sympathize with the younger brother. We see ourselves as sinners having returned to God. But if you have been raised in the church, you may be more like the elder brother than the younger. If so, you will see if you read carefully that you are in danger of losing your Father's inheritance.

Jesus' stories and teaching are full of surprises, surprises that lead to self-knowledge for us, the readers of the Gospels. We read to find out who Jesus is and we discover that he knows precisely who we are! So as we read about Jesus, we are led further and further into his character. We see more and more of who he is, and we either fall in love with him and become his disciples or, like the rich young ruler in Luke 18:18-30, we go away sad.

To become a Christian is to become a disciple of Christ, a follower of him as Lord. It is to develop a personal relationship with the very Lord of the Universe. In doing so, we begin to imitate our Master. This is an awesome task, and impossible if it were not for the Holy Spirit.

The Spirit of Christ himself comes to live within us. Jesus, then, is both the author and the finisher of our faith—the one who comes to us, saves us by his death on the cross, transforms us gradually into the person we really are when we are right with God, and empowers us to live holy lives in a broken world. We will see something of how this comes about in the next chapter. In the parable the neighbor is not the man in the ditch. It is the Samaritan himself who proves to be the neighbor. The Jew is to act like the Samaritan, not like a Jew.

QUESTIONS FOR REFLECTION

1. What was your view of Jesus before you began reading this book? Has your understanding changed? How?

2. Read the account of Jesus healing the paralyzed man in Mark 2:2-12. Had you been in the crowd surrounding Jesus, what would have struck you most—his healing of the paralyzed man or his forgiving the man's sins? Why?

3. How does Jesus' declaration, "Son, your sins are forgiven," imply a claim to a special relationship to God?

4. If Jesus did not have the authority to forgive sins and he knew it, what kind of a person was he? If he thought he had the authority but didn't, what kind of person was he? Do either of these options—liar or seriously self-deluded—seem characteristic of Jesus as he is described in other parts of the Gospels?

5. If Jesus had the power to forgive sins, what is the most reasonable response we can make to him today?

6. In the story of the prodigal son, who are you most like? The father, younger son, or older son? Explain your choice.

7. What did the younger son learn? What was the father trying to teach the older son? At the end of the parable, what choice did the father force the elder son to make? Why do you think the Gospel writer did not tell us what the elder son decided to do?

8. Where do you now stand in relation to Jesus? On the basis of these two main stories—a healing narrative and a parable—what will you do differently?

CHAPTER THIRTEEN

God's Forever Family

At the round earths imagin'd corners, blow
Your trumpets, Angells, and arise, arise
From death, you numberlesse infinities
Of soules, and to your scattered bodies goe,
All whom the flood did, and fire shall overthrow,
All whom warre, death, age, agues, tyrannies,
Despair, law, chance, hath slaine, and you whose eyes,
Shall behold God, and never tast death's woe.

JOHN DONNE, "HOLY SONNET VII," LINES 1-8

IN THE LATE 1960S at the height of student unrest, a group of Christians in Berkeley, California, banded together to show that God was even more concerned for justice, peace, and freedom than the most radical of the radicals. The group had a variety of names, but one of them comes as close to defining the church in general as any I can think of. They called themselves God's Forever Family.

This is indeed what Christians are: members of God's family from now through eternity.

Remember the first question we asked at the opening of the book: Who am I? We have come

a long way since then. We now can see ourselves
as Christians—men and women not only made in
the image of God and fallen (as all people are)
but also as redeemed and now in the process
of restoration.

In earlier chapters we have largely been concerned about the broken relationship between
God and us as human beings. We have thus focused on the vertical dimension of Christian life.
But, as we saw in chapter six, when Adam and
Eve disobeyed God, they also fell out with one
another, Adam blaming Eve for his own decision.
When two children came to the first pair, one of
them murdered the other. And so it has been
throughout ensuing generations. We need,
therefore, a healing of broken horizontal relation-
ships as well as broken vertical ones.

Part of the image of God is our maleness and
femaleness. When found in harmony, this reflects
the corporate nature of the Trinity as Father, Son,
and Holy Spirit. When restoration comes in a
Christian's life, therefore, it has a corporate dimension. As children of the Father we are brothers
and sisters in Christ. We are God's family. And as
a family that extends from the new birth through
to eternity, we are God's *forever* family.

Even now, before glorification in the City of
God, we reflect something of what is to come.

As John writes, "Dear friends, now we are children of God, and what we will be has not yet been made known. But we know that when Christ appears, we shall be like him, for we shall see him as he is" (1 John 3:2). And thus as his family we corporately display the *already but not yet* of the kingdom of God (now in part but still coming in fullness).

WE ARE ONE

The New Testament uses many images to picture the church. Peter strings together four of them in the following verse: "You are a chosen race, a royal priesthood, a holy nation, God's own people, that you may declare the wonderful deeds of him who called you out of darkness into his marvelous light" (1 Peter 2:9, NIV 1984). Let's look at each image in turn.

A chosen race. God chose us from many "races" to be a single *race*. Notice the corporate nature of all these images: *race, priesthood, nation,* and *people.* Here the emphasis is on the fact of being chosen. God in his divine sovereignty has come to us. He took the initiative while Moses was out in the wilderness and while we were yet sinners.

A royal priesthood. Regal imagery abounds throughout the New Testament. We are said to be citizens of the kingdom of God. Here we are not just ordinary people but royal priests. God is King; we are priests who stand, therefore, before God without any other mediator than Jesus Christ, God the Son. This notion supplants the whole sacrificial system of the Old Testament, for the ultimate sacrifice has been made. This allows for the priesthood of all believers.

A holy nation. Holy means "separated" and is associated with the notion of righteousness. As Christians our nation is set off from all others, reflecting in its separateness the separateness of God, and in its righteousness the righteousness of God.

God's own people. In the Old Testament the people of God were the nation of Israel. In the New Testament the people of God are all those who trust Christ as their Savior and Lord. God's people, family, nation, and race knows no human "tribal," "racial," or "national" boundaries. Just as "from one man he made all the nations, that they should inhabit the whole earth" (Acts 17:26), he makes one out of all individual believers from all over the world.

As the apostle Paul puts it, "There is one body and one Spirit, just as you were called to one hope when you were called; one Lord, one faith, one baptism; one God and Father of all, who is over all and through all and in all" (Ephesians 4:4-6).

WE ARE MANY

As we have seen many times in our investigation of the Christian faith, one truth is usually balanced by another. The truth of the corporate nature of the church is balanced by the truth of its variegated character. The church is not like a bowl of mush with every scoop the same. It is more like a Persian rug, which, though almost infinite in variety, is yet one single whole.

This balance is captured in Paul's description of spiritual gifts in the church:

> There are different kinds of gifts, but the same Spirit distributes them. There are different kinds of service, but the same Lord. There are different kinds of working, but in all of them and in everyone it is the same God at work.
>
> Now to each one the manifestation of the Spirit is given for the common good. To one there is given through the Spirit a message of wisdom, to another a message of knowledge by means of the same Spirit, to another faith by the same Spirit, to another gifts of healing by that one Spirit, to another miraculous powers, to another prophecy, to another distinguishing between spirits, to another speaking in different kinds of tongues, and to still another the

interpretation of tongues. All these are the work of one and the same Spirit, and he distributes them to each one, just as he determines. (1 Corinthians 12:4-11)

Individual Christians have specific and limited gifts. Though it is one Spirit who gives the gifts, and though the gifts are for the "common good" (not for the one with the gift but for his brothers and sisters in Christ), each person is unique. In genuine Christian communities individuals are not reduced to the lowest common denominator of the group but are encouraged to develop and express their specific gifts for the benefit of all. Paul develops this notion in the next few verses:

Just as a body, though one, has many parts, but all its many parts form one body, so it is with Christ. For we were all baptized by one Spirit so as to form one body—whether Jews or Gentiles, slave or free—and we were all given the one Spirit to drink. Even so the body is not made up of one part but of many.

Now if the foot should say, "Because I am not a hand, I do not belong to the body," it would not for that reason stop being part of the body. And if the ear should say, "Because I am not an eye, I do not belong to the body," it would not for that reason stop being part of the body. If the whole body were an eye, where would the sense of hearing be? If the whole body were an ear, where would the sense of smell be? But in fact God has placed the parts in the body, every one of them, just as he wanted them to be. If they were all one part, where would the body be? As it is, there are many parts, but one body.

The eye cannot say to the hand, "I don't need you!" And the head cannot say to the feet, "I don't need you!" . . . If one part suffers, every part suffers with it; if one part is honored, every part rejoices with it. (1 Corinthians 12:12-21, 26)

Think of any genuinely Christian group. In it there will be those to whom God has given the ability to teach. They are wise in their judgment, and, while they too make mistakes, we recognize in them a special ability or talent to explain Scripture to the rest of us. In my own local congregation there are, as Paul puts it, people with hands who are especially able to help others. Some with feet provide transportation for those without cars. Some with discerning eyes see the needs of others. Some with sensitive ears hear the pleas for help that are often masked by small talk and flip remarks. And all of us need each other. We are one body.

As in the Trinity, so in the church: not only is there unity in diversity, but diversity in unity as well. And that is what makes God's forever family a reflection even now of what is yet to be when we are fully restored in God's image and transformed like Jesus after his resurrection.

AT THE END OF HISTORY

When Jesus ascended to his Father, the messengers said we would see him returning in the same way we saw him go (Acts 1:11). Of course, that hasn't happened yet.

We are now in the middle of things. God has saved us from the consequences of sin; he is saving us from the power of sin; he has yet to save us from the presence of sin. But it is this latter toward which we look. What do we know of how this will happen or when?

The when is easy to answer. We know we will not know until it happens. Jesus himself told his followers, "It is not for you to know the times or dates the Father has set by his own authority" (Acts 1:7; also Matthew 24:36). Christ will rather come "like a thief in the night" (1 Thessalonians 5:2; Luke 12:39-40). We, therefore, should be ready for his coming at any time.

Jesus told the parable of the ten virgins for just this purpose (Matthew 25:1–13). When the bridegroom came, five had oil in their lamps and five did not. By the time the negligent five had secured oil, it was too late. They knocked on the door, saying "Lord, Lord, open the door to us." But he answered, "Truly, I tell you, I don't know you." Jesus commented on this parable, "Therefore keep watch, because you do not know the day or the hour."

While we do not know the time, we do know something about what the events will be. The Son of God will return in a visible way. The dead in Christ will be resurrected, taking spiritual bodies presumably after the manner of Jesus after his resurrection (1 Corinthians 15). Those who are alive will be caught up with them "to meet the Lord in the air" (1 Thessalonians 4:16-17). Everyone will be judged (Matthew 25:31-46), and those who are God's people will inherit "the kingdom prepared for [them] since the creation of the world" (Matthew 25:34). Those who are not his people will "go away to eternal punishment" (Matthew 25:46).

Many Christians believe, on the basis of the book of Revelation and related biblical prophecy, that Christ will reign with his people for a thousand years (a millennium) here on earth (Revelation 20:4-6). Others hold that this is a symbol of

God's reign among his people now. Still others have worked out elaborate charts that, while they contain no dates, do outline in subtle detail the order of events as they believe the Bible says they will take place.

Certainly there is in Scripture much more about the end times than we have space to examine here. I will simply direct your attention to some of the more relevant biblical passages. Jesus' Olivet discourse, Matthew 24-26 (with parallels in Mark 13 and Luke 21) contains much of Jesus' own teaching. Both of Paul's Letters to the Thessalonians, who seem to have been troubled with such questions, contain some of Paul's most explicit remarks (1 Thessalonians 4:13–5:11; 2 Thessalonians 2:1-12). 1 Corinthians 15 is the most elaborate teaching about the resurrection of the body. And, of course, the Revelation to John is a vision, puzzling to be sure, of what is and what is to take place hereafter (Revelation 1:19). I have mentioned in the notes a few books by modern biblical scholars that may also be helpful.

A GLIMPSE OF GLORY

However the events of the end times unfold, it is surely appropriate to end our summary and study of basic Christianity with John's vision of the new Jerusalem.

If God brought the universe into existence by his word of power some vague and distant time in the past, it is also true that this universe will one day pass out of existence. The people he has made in his image, then redeemed and restored to his image, will live forever with him. What will this life be like? We have only a glimpse, but enough to give us hope and, even now in the *already but not yet,* to bring us great joy.

Then I saw "a new heaven and a new earth," for the first heaven and the first earth had passed away, and there was no longer any sea. I saw the Holy City, the new Jerusalem, coming down out of heaven from God, prepared as a bride beautifully dressed for her husband. And I heard a loud voice from the throne saying, "Look! God's dwelling place is now among the people, and he will dwell with them. They will be his people, and God himself will be with them and be their God. 'He will wipe every tear from their eyes. There will be no more death' or mourning or crying or pain, for the old order of things has passed away." . . . I did not see a temple in the city, because the Lord God Almighty and the Lamb are its temple. The city does not need the sun or the moon to shine on it, for the glory of God gives it light, and the Lamb is its lamp. The nations will walk by its light, and the kings of the earth will bring their splendor into it. On no day will its gates ever be shut, for there will be no night there. The glory and honor of the nations will be brought into it. Nothing impure will ever enter it, nor will anyone who does what is shameful or deceitful, but only those whose names are written in the Lamb's book of life. (Revelation 21:1-4, 22-27)

May the words at the close of Revelation (22:20) be our prayer: "Amen. Come, Lord Jesus."

QUESTIONS FOR REFLECTION

1. Why is *God's forever family* an apt phrase for the church?

2. How does the church help us express and fulfill the image of God that is being restored in us?

3. How does the church reflect the *already but not yet* status of Christians?

4. How is the church one? Why is it one?

5. How is the church diverse? Why should it be?

6. What limits are placed on both oneness and diversity in the church?

7. Explain the four images of the church in 1 Peter 2:9.

8. What is in store for Christians in the future?

9. Study Matthew 24:36, Luke 12:39-40, Acts 1:7, Acts 1:11, and 1 Thessalonians 5:2. What do they add to your knowledge of the end times?

10. Reflect on Revelation 21:1-4, 22-27. Share your reflections with God in prayer.

Notes

CHAPTER ONE: WHAT'S IN A NAME?

15 The study of names is a complex field. Our discussion barely scratches the surface. For further background you will find many books in your local library and plenty of information on the internet. For a simple, basic survey, try Eloise Lambert and Mario Pei, *Our Names: Where They Came From and What They Mean* (New York: Lothrop, Lee, and Shephard, 1960). For the meanings of many surnames, see Basil Cottle, *The Penguin Dictionary of Surnames* (Baltimore: Penguin, 1967). Two more scholarly and detailed works of considerable interest are J. R. Dolan, *English Ancestral Names: The Evolution of the Surname from Medieval Occupations* (New York: Clarkson N. Potter, 1972), and George R. Stewart, *American Given Names* (New York: Oxford University Press, 1979). Stewart makes an interesting observation about the name Alice. Deriving from the same original as Adelaide (Germanic form *athal*, "noble," and *naidu*, "kind, soft"), the name was popular in the middle ages, then fell largely into disuse. In the nineteenth century it

revived in popularity due in part to a romantic return to the past and in part to the popularity of Lewis Carroll's *Alice's Adventures in Wonderland and Through the Looking-Glass* (New York: P. F. Collier & Son, 1903), 242. By 1900 Alice was second only to Mary in numbers. Apparently, readers did not agree with Humpty Dumpty's dour analysis of the name.

CHAPTER TWO: BEGINNING WITH GOD

32 The two God and creation diagrams are adapted from Francis Schaeffer, *The God Who Is There* (Downers Grove, IL: InterVarsity Press, 1968), 94-95.

34 The question of the meaning of the image of God has been much debated over the centuries. I have found the following publications helpful in clarifying the view expressed in this chapter: Ranald Macaulay and Jerram Barrs, "In the Likeness of God," in *Being Human: The Nature of Spiritual Experience* (Downers Grove, IL: InterVarsity Press, 1978), 11-27; William Dyrness, "Man and Woman," in *Themes in Old Testament Theology* (Downers Grove, IL: InterVarsity Press, 1979), 79-96; James M. Houston, *I Believe in the Creator* (Grand Rapids: Eerdmans, 1980), 72-82; E. H. Merrill, "Image of God," in *Dictionary of the Old Testament: Pentateuch*, ed. T. Desmond Alexander and

David W. Baker (Downers Grove, IL: InterVarsity Press, 2003), 441-45.

CHAPTER FOUR: THE GOD WHO IS

54 Perhaps the most simply profound books on the doctrine of God are David Bentley Hart, *The Experience of God* (New Haven, CT: Yale University Press, 2013), and J. I. Packer, *Knowing God* (Downers Grove, IL: InterVarsity Press, 1973). I have also found the discussions in the following books quite helpful: Donald G. Bloesch, *Essentials of Evangelical Theology*, vol. 1 (San Francisco: Harper & Row, 1978), esp. "The Sovereignty of God," 24-50; J. Oliver Buswell, *A Systematic Theology of the Christian Religion* (Grand Rapids: Zondervan, 1962), 29-129.

54 The hymn "Immortal, Invisible, God Only Wise" (1867) is by Walter Chalmers Smith.

58 The quotation from Geoffrey Bromiley is from *Baker's Dictionary of Theology*, ed. Everett F. Harrison, Geoffrey Bromiley, and Carl F. H. Henry (Grand Rapids: Baker, 1960), 531.

65 The poem is from Alexander Pope, *An Essay on Man* (London: John Sharpe, 1828), 10.

CHAPTER FIVE: MAN AND WOMAN

67 The quotation from *Pensées* is from Blaise Pascal, *Thoughts, Letters & Minor Works* (New York: Cosimo Classics, 1910), 136.

CHAPTER SIX: THE BAD NEWS
ABOUT HUMAN BEINGS

77   John Murray and B. A. Milne's entry on "sin"
     in the *New Bible Dictionary*, 3rd ed. (Downers
     Grove, IL: InterVarsity Press, 1996), 1105-09,
     gives a broad analysis of the concept, tracing
     its definition, origin, and consequences, and
     also discusses imputation, depravity, human
     inability, and liability. William Dyrness's
     chapter on sin in *Themes in Old Testament
     Theology* (Downers Grove, IL: InterVarsity
     Press, 1980), and H. A. G. Blocher, "Sin," in
     New Dictionary of Biblical Theology, ed.
     T. Desmond Alexander, Brian S. Rosner,
     D. A. Carson, and Graeme Goldsworthy
     (Downers Grove, IL: InterVarsity Press, 2000),
     781-88 are also worth consulting.

77   The quotation from John Milton is from *Paradise Lost* (New York: Baker and Scribner,
     1851), 398.

CHAPTER SEVEN: SIN

89   The quotation from *Pensées* is from Blaise
     Pascal, *Thoughts, Letters & Minor Works*
     (New York: Cosimo Classics, 1910), 147.

90   The definition of sin from John Murray is found
     in the *New Bible Dictionary*, third ed. (Downers
     Grove, IL: InterVarsity Press, 1996). Concerning
     the money given to God (Mk 7:11), see R. Alan
     Cole in *The Gospel According to St. Mark: An*

Introduction and Commentary (Grand Rapids: Eerdmans, 1969), 119.

CHAPTER EIGHT: GOD IN SEARCH OF HIS PEOPLE

100 I have found especially helpful the brief summary of Old Testament history in William Wells, *Welcome to the Family: An Introduction to Evangelical Christianity* (Downers Grove, IL: InterVarsity Press, 1979), 46-51. The chart on page 108 is adapted from Wells and used with his and the publisher's permission. John Stott retells the history of the Old and New Testament in two long chapters in *Understanding the Bible* (Glendale, CA: Regal Books, 1972), 59-158. For more detail, however, I suggest Samuel J. Schultz, *The Old Testament Speaks* (New York: Harper, 1960); it is a masterful survey of the flow of Old Testament history. *The New Bible Dictionary*, 3rd ed. (Downers Grove, IL: InterVarsity Press, 1996) entries "The Chronology of the Old Testament" and "The Chronology of the New Testament," 188-89, are also useful. See also Tremper Longman III, *Old Testament Essentials: Creation, Conquest, Exile and Return* (Downers Grove, IL: InterVarsity Press, 2013); Robbie Fox Castleman, *New Testament Essentials: Father, Son, Spirit and Kingdom* (Downers Grove, IL: InterVarsity Press, 2014); and Sandra L. Richter, *The Epic of*

Eden: A Christian Entry into the Old Testament (Downers Grove, IL: InterVarsity Press, 2008).

100   The quotation from Robert Farrar Capon is from *An Offering of Uncles*, in *The Romance of the Word* (Grand Rapids: Eerdmans, 1995), 51.

100   The quotation from John Milton is from *Paradise Lost* (New York: Baker and Scribner, 1851), 536.

CHAPTER NINE: GOD'S FINISHED WORK

115   This chapter barely scratches the surface of the meaning of redemption. For more of the Bible's own words, read Romans (especially chapters 1–8) and Paul's letter to the Galatians. J. I. Packer's chapter 18, "The Heart of the Gospel," in *Knowing God* (Downers Grove, IL: InterVarsity Press, 1973), is also helpful, as are earlier chapters on God's justice, wrath, goodness, and severity (chaps. 14–16). See also Timothy Keller, *The Prodigal God: Recovering the Heart of the Christian Faith* (New York: Dutton, 2008), and James Choung, *True Story: A Christianity Worth Believing In* (Downers Grove, IL: InterVarsity Press, 2008).

115   The quotation from John White is from *The Fight* (Downers Grove, IL: InterVarsity Press, 1976), 87-88.

120   The quotation from John Milton is from *Paradise Lost* (New York: Baker and Scribner, 1851), 125.

CHAPTER TEN: NEW LIFE IN CHRIST

124   It is helpful to have available (for yourself and for others you may speak to about spiritual matters) a handy summary of what is involved in becoming a Christian. I recommend especially the straightforward presentation by John Stott in the small booklet *Becoming a Christian*, updated ed. (Downers Grove, IL: InterVarsity Press, 2016). See also James Choung, *Real Life: A Christianity Worth Living Out* (Downers Grove, IL: InterVarsity Press, 2012), and N. T. Wright, *Simply Christian: Why Christianity Makes Sense* (HarperSanFrancisco, 2006).

124   The poem is from John Donne, *The Divine Poems of John Donne*, ed. Helen Gardner (Oxford: Oxford University Press, 1955), 12.

CHAPTER ELEVEN: A NEW LIFESTYLE

139   There are many excellent books on the Christian life. At the top of the list I would place John White's *The Fight* (Downers Grove, IL: InterVarsity Press, 1976), which covers many basic aspects: prayer, Bible study, knowing God's will, and handling temptation, among others. A more elaborate practical theology of new life in Christ is found in Ranald Macaulay and Jerram Barrs's *Being Human: The Nature of Spiritual Experience* (Downers Grove, IL: InterVarsity Press, 1978). Francis Schaeffer in *The Mark of the Christian*, 2nd ed. (Downers Grove, IL:

InterVarsity Press, 2006) focuses on love as the central character of the Christian life. Hazel Offner, *The Fruit of the Spirit* (Downers Grove, IL: InterVarsity Press, 1977) is a Bible study guide to each of the fruits mentioned by Paul in Galatians 5:22-23. In *Faith That Works* (Downers Grove, IL: InterVarsity Press, 1981), Andrew and Phyllis Le Peau take readers through the book of James in eleven Bible studies. For Bible study in general I suggest T. Norton Sterret and Richard L. Schultz, *How to Understand Your Bible*, 3rd ed. (Downers Grove, IL: InterVarsity Press, 2010).

144   The comment by John Stott on Galatians 5:21 derives from his *Only One Way: The Message of Galatians* (Downers Grove, IL: InterVarsity Press, 1968), 148.

CHAPTER TWELVE: JESUS THE CHRIST

152   Every chapter in this book calls out for expansion, but especially this one. And there are many books that will do so. Still, I urge readers first to read, reread, and meditate on the four Gospels of Matthew, Mark, Luke, and John. Then extend your reading to such basic books as John Stott, *Basic Christianity*, 50th anniv. ed. (Downers Grove, IL: InterVarsity Press, 2012). This book is a masterful explanation of Christianity from the point of view of the identity of Jesus. Two other books that will further expand your general grasp of

Jesus are Philip Yancey, *The Jesus I Never Knew* (Grand Rapids: Zondervan, 1995), and James Choung, *True Story: A Christianity Worth Believing In* (Downers Grove, IL: InterVarsity Press, 2008). Two especially helpful books on Jesus' parables are Helmut Thielicke, *The Waiting Father*, trans. John W. Doberstein (New York: Harper & Brothers, 1959), and Kenneth E. Bailey, *Poet and Peasant* and *Through Peasant Eyes* (a double volume) (Grand Rapids: William B. Eerdmans, 1983).

154   For an analysis of the historical reliability of the Gospel records, see R. T. France, *The Evidence for Jesus* (Downers Grove, IL: InterVarsity Press, 1986); Paul Barnett, *Is the New Testament Reliable: A Look at the Historical Evidence* (Downers Grove, IL: InterVarsity Press, 1986); Michael J. Wilkins and J. P. Moreland, *Jesus Under Fire: Modern Scholarship Reinvents the Historical Jesus* (Grand Rapids: Zondervan, 1995); and Craig L. Blomberg, *The Historical Reliability of the Gospels*, 2nd ed. (Downers Grove, IL: InterVarsity Press, 2007). One of the most thorough, scholarly studies of Jesus is N. T. Wright's massive trilogy Christian Origins and the Question of God, 3 vols. (Minneapolis: Fortress Press): *Jesus and the Victory of God* (1996), *The New Testament and the People of God* (1992), and *The Resurrection and the Son of God* (2017). Finally, getting back to basics,

read my own group Bible study guide, *Jesus the Reason* (Downers Grove, IL: InterVarsity Press, 1996), which presents eight Bible studies designed for groups and individual seekers and new believers.

CHAPTER THIRTEEN: GOD'S FOREVER FAMILY

166   The poem is from John Donne, *The Divine Poems of John Donne*, ed. Helen Gardner (Oxford: Oxford University Press, 1955), 8.

166   The phrase *God's forever family* dates to the late 1960s and derives, as far as I know, from the Christians in Berkeley associated with the Christian World Liberation Front. Their story is told by one of their leaders, Jack Sparks, in *God's Forever Family* (Grand Rapids: Zondervan, 1974).

170   There are many excellent books on the nature and character of the church and of the spiritual gifts. I will mention two that I have found helpful: Howard Snyder, *The Problem of Wineskins* (Downers Grove, IL: InterVarsity Press, 1975); and Bruce Milne, *We Belong Together* (Downers Grove, IL: InterVarsity Press, 1978).

173   On eschatology—the doctrine of the end times—see "Eschatology" in *The New Bible Dictionary*, 3rd ed. (Downers Grove, IL: InterVarsity Press, 1996), 333-39; and K. E. Brower, "Eschatology," *in New Dictionary of Biblical Theology*, ed. T. Desmond Alexander, Brian

S. Rosner, D. A. Carson, and Graeme Golds-
worthy (Downers Grove, IL: InterVarsity Press,
2000), 459-64. Robert Clouse, ed. *The
Meaning of the Millennium: Four Views*
(Downers Grove, IL: InterVarsity Press, 1977)
presents the cases for and against four specific ways to understand the thousand years
mentioned in Revelation 20:4-6. For a bril-
liant, imaginative view of what is in store for
humanity, read C. S. Lewis, *The Great Divorce*
(New York: Macmillan, 1946).

Other Books
by James W. Sire